Good God?

Good God?

God-Poisoning and God-Images

ROSEMARIE KÖHN AND SUSANNE SØNDERBO

TRANSLATED BY OTTO CHRISTENSEN

WIPF & STOCK · Eugene, Oregon

GOOD GOD?
God-Poisoning and God-Images

Copyright © 2009 Rosemarie Köhn and Susanne Sønderbo. All rights reserved. Except for brief quotations in critical publications or reviews, no part of this book may be reproduced in any manner without prior written permission from the publisher. Write: Permissions, Wipf and Stock Publishers, 199 W. 8th Ave., Suite 3, Eugene, OR 97401.

English language translation by Otto Christensen
English Translation Copyright © 2007, Wipf and Stock Publishers. Originally published as *Gode Gud? Gudsforgiftning Og Gudsbilder,* Pax Forlag A/S, Oslo 2003. All Rights Reserved.

Wipf & Stock
A Division of Wipf and Stock Publishers
199 W. 8th Ave., Suite 3
Eugene, OR 97401
www.wipfandstock.com

ISBN 13: 978-1-55635-559-2

Manufactured in the U.S.A.

Scripture quotations in the English language translation are from the New Revised Standard Version of the Bible, copyright © 1989 by the Division of Christian Education of the National Council of Churches of Christ in the USA, and are used by permission.

Other copyrighted material used in this book gratefully acknowledged and used by permission in the original Norwegian version.

*Ari, Nik, Helga, Kristinn,
Mark, Thomas, Miriam and Daniel*

*that each may know by experience
that the universal language of love
makes the dream of a shared harmonious world
a joyful reality.*

Contents

Foreword ix
Preface xv

1 Godpoisoning 1
2 *Image of God* 7
3 God-images and God-representation 12
4 Personality Development and Faith Development 21
5 The *Image of God* and the Debate over Same-sex Partnership 46
6 Destructive Religion 76
7 "The Exact Imprint of God's Very Being"—Matthew's Jesus 88
8 A Good, Life-giving *Image of God* 113

Bibliography 151

Multicultural Universalist Spirituality

Foreword to a Norwegian book about growth
—by Canadian translator

Not that we are what we eat, but our eating habits and choices tell a story: Pancakes and lingonberries for breakfast with coffee or tea, of course. Borscht and curried chicken for lunch. For supper it's pizza and a Mexican beer. And for night snack we may have plantain chips and green tea.

Today we live the story of excited taste buds and pluralism—a world expanding in culture and exploding in choices and options. A tremendously exciting world.

My mother's most exciting food adventure was buying a case of Jaffa grapefruits in January one year. Although she and my father did lots of holiday traveling and were exposed to different foods they loved coming home to real food, which to them was lots of potatoes, meat and gravy.

In North America multiculturalism is the order of the day. In Canada it is written into the constitution and bilingualism is government policy. United States is the big melting pot. The American Dream of prosperity and independence created a unified culture in kind. On the other hand U.S. culture is perhaps better described as a smorgasbord of choices: ethnic, religious, economic, lifestyle, education etc. It almost seems that the unifying culture is the one of having as many choices as possible. Having no choice or only few choices is not the American Way! It is almost equal to decline, doom and disaster.

The world of choice defines who we are as human beings. Yet we who live with all these choices still have a yearning for monoculture and a simple life. One GOD of all. One Destiny. One Future. One Humanity. Living in North America in an affluent society we are stretched between extreme individualism and the hope for a homogenous society. In his second inaugural address George W Bush spoke about United States as a super agent for freedom around the world. At times the 'American Way' is seen as the only way. And the smug Canadian says "Those Americans!"

Our quest for the ultimate good—the religious quest of all times—so easily becomes identical with the one thing we know and love. In religious fashion we start to promote our own way of life sometimes to the exclusion of and in disrespect of any other. The disastrous results are only too well known from our history and from the present conflicts around the world. Religion and culture are so interwoven that to most people no distinction is made. Still culture changes with time. Religion likewise. There is a dynamic relationship between the two.

"It's all the same GOD anyway," say the people. I have heard this both in the coffee shop and in the counseling room. Most often it has been said to me as a disclaimer. "Please leave me alone. I'm comfortable with my *image of God* the way it is. There is no need for conversion."

In situations like that I have felt cautious. Talking about God is difficult. Our *image of God* is colored by our cultural experience, age, gender, skin color and a number of personal factors and choices. Further it is a very right brain activity to talk about our *image of God*. Experience tells us that the *image of God* we carry is a reflection of how we have been influenced from birth until the present. Amazing! Our *image of God* then is a conglomerate of all that we have been exposed to and endowed with—stored in the file folder named "GOD". It would be a grand error to confuse our *image of God* with anything that might be GOD self. This said without prejudice. The philosophical question of GOD's existence is separate from the awareness each person has of GOD.

Perhaps this introduction makes it clear that talking about GOD easily creates more confusion than clarity. This is precisely why the book you hold in your hands is helpful. Köhn and Sønderbo wrote the book from the perspective of a common frame of reference, namely our *image of God*—yours and mine. They suggest any talk about GOD needs to start with sharing our individualized *image of God*. It is so much better to share our personal stories than to exchange impersonal views on the topic. The book does just that.

When we use phrases such as "the will of God," "God's word," "God forbid!" etc. they tend to signify the end of the conversation. It is as if the person were to say: "There is nothing more to talk about! I have this from

Foreword

God self. Nothing can be more authoritative." This book wants to move us further into a conversation about GOD. Behind this goal there is a belief in continuous growth. A belief I support. I believe my personal growth in faith is nurtured by a continuing dialogue with self and others. Reading this book in a way gave me new excitement about the goodness of life for all. So much that I saw it fit to share it with readers in the English speaking world as well. Therefore it is designed to reach all of us who are on a life long journey of faith towards wholeness with GOD, self and community. This book is good food for the journey.

Exploring "truth" together is paramount. Entering and continuing a conversation with no foregone conclusion is the way out of conflict and pain. In the interest of cooperation and co-existence—a world with room for all views—it is absolutely necessary to go behind the words and explore new levels of understanding.

This of course is a value laden statement—an opinion if you like. I have no problem admitting this. I am willing to debate it. I may be convinced that there is a better way to look at the world, but for now this is my motivation for inventing new language and adopting new virtues. Perhaps in the process we may discover that the new was already in the old—only that we didn't look deep enough at first.

At one time we were advised to keep our conversation away from religion, politics and sex. That is if you wanted to be politically correct, safe, and uncontroversial. I plead a case for the opposite. Superficial harmony is dangerous, and can erupt into open conflict at any time. A better way of dealing with differences in opinion is by honest self-examination and common sharing of our hopes and dreams. This is actually the way North America was settled: pushing the frontier of discovery all the way across the continent. I do not mean to imply that people have to be won over to a different way (converted). I advocate an open dialogue in the interest of becoming more human and inclusive.

Sexuality for example is experienced in a variety of ways. In a multicultural society sexual expressions are bound to be multiple also. Offensive clothing? Same gender partnership? Sexually transmitted diseases? Sex for profit? Sex for pleasure? It is hard to define common values about sex. So hard that we need to accept the multiplicity of views. The alternative would be harassment, discrimination or elimination—perhaps by sending people to extermination camp. It has been done even in recent history.

Foreword

Bone chilling stories provide a reality check for anyone who thinks that a little bit of discrimination is acceptable and not dangerous.

In the spiritual realm we have come to the point where talking about GOD becomes a "supremacy-talk". This is not helpful for cooperation between nations, individuals, or groups of individuals. As we choose cooperation we must accept human diversity.

I grew up in Denmark and spent nine years in Nigeria before coming to Canada in 1989. My personal experience in cross-cultural living is the platform from which I draw my values. Others have arrived at this differently. Together we believe variety and multiplicity enrich our lives.

My first year in Canada I learned a rhyme from Icelandic-Canadian farmer and poet Brandur Finnsson. Interesting how something said at a time when you are receptive stays with you forever. His words are still very clear to me.

I care not much for the Catholic God, his creed is so disciplinary.
I much better like the Lutheran God who allows all his clergymen to marry.
And then there is the freewheeling federated God, a friend to all in daily hassle.
But the God I love best . . . is the GOD with whom I can wrestle.

In the history of the Christian Church denominationalism is a modern day phenomenon. Multiculturalism and a world of choices are also new. Further it is for the privileged 15–20% of the world population. My point is that in our world of multiple options and choices as a point of maturity we similarly need to embrace the philosophy of equality. It is not for me to pass judgment! In fact it is already built into the culture in the form of prevalence. All religions are foremost concerned with a personal growth in faith, and recognize that a neighbour's faith is equally sacred. Growth implies change; and growth is nurtured by soulful sharing.

A story comes to mind from the time when the Christian religion started to separate itself from Judaism: The apostles were cross-examined by the Jewish religious authorities and one who was respected by all the people, Gamaliel, gave his time honored advice: "If this plan or this undertaking is of human origin, it will fail. But if it is of GOD, you will not be able to overthrow them—in that case you may even be found fighting against GOD!" Add to this now that our biggest challenge as a

Foreword

global society is cooperation, co-existence and being neighbours—soulful neighbors jointly exploring the ultimate good of all.

I am grateful for how my life has been nurtured by soulful sharing in a supportive community within the Christian tradition. I need not convert to a new religion. But I do need to keep my focus on growth and maturity and take in the riches of the ages, cultures and individuals who also travel towards wholeness of life. I am in good company. So are you, the reader. This book invites you to take time and effort—perhaps with a group of friends—to get to know yourself and your own endowed *image of God* . . . and perhaps in the process catch a glimpse of GOD self as GOD passes by while you grow.

Practically speaking we had trouble with the word: GOD or God or god. In Jewish tradition you not even *write* the name of the divine. However we chose a traditional way.

Same sex partnership becomes a testing point for inclusivity. How inclusive should we be? It seems to me that inclusive cannot be conjugated. It is or it isn't. Like it is with GOD, God, god!

GOOD?

Enough said. Enjoy your reading!

Otto Christensen,
Spiritual Care Coordinator,
Interlake Regional Health Authority
Arborg, Manitoba, Canada.
June 21, 2008

Preface

OUR *IMAGE OF GOD*—WHAT is it? How did we get it? Is it like a sandcastle, easily washed away when the waters rise and the waves roll over it? Or is it more like a concrete structure—poured into a mould and we are stuck with it for a lifetime? Is a certain *image of God* better than another? How do we evaluate our *image of God*?

Virtually every person has what may be called an "*image of God*"—an emotional picture of GOD. We may be aware of it, but more often we are not. This *image of God* is an integral part of a person's faith, the essence of which is to guide the person, adding meaning and purpose to life. But a person's faith can also become toxic and result in self degradation, a false sense of guilt, and feelings of hatred towards others especially those with a different belief or life style. Godpoisoning is a term used here for the case when a person becomes stuck on a negative *image of God*. A distorted *image of God* arises when a single aspect or attribute of GOD is overemphasized or absolutized. In the extreme case this results in psychosocial or mental illness.

Our intention with this book is to raise our collective and individual consciousness in regards to our *image of God*, and to facilitate reflections about this. Perhaps even to help someone get a more nuanced *image of God*. It is not uncommon to mistake ones own *image of God* for GOD. Neither is it uncommon to shy away from self-examination when it comes to our *image of God*. An important aspect of this book is to explore how our *image of God* is established in early childhood and how it may or may not be susceptible to development and change (sandcastle vs. concrete). Erik Erikson's developmental psychology forms the basis for an expanded theory on development beyond the age of 56 (the last age of Erikson's theory). Based on Erikson's developmental ages we suggest that it is indeed possible to have a life long spiritual growth—a sort of 'coming home to your authentic self'.

Preface

Further we attempt to fit in a specific approach to the *image of God* as it is used in the Christian tradition by the New Testament writers who name the person Jesus to be "The *image of God*". To illustrate this you are invited into the gallery of St. Matthew's Gospel for a tour of nine images—vignettes.

We write this book based on our educational and professional backgrounds. Susanne Sønderbo—trained and employed in psychology—leading retreats, providing therapy for many years and then entering pastoral ministry and hospital chaplaincy. Rosemarie Köhn—the pastor, teacher and theologian—doing research in Old Testament and Hebrew and later in New Testament Theology, becoming the first female bishop in Norway. Perhaps you will find the terminology used in the book a bit more professional than you like. This being said, the intention is to move the conversation away from the trivial and into an arena of inter-disciplinary professionalism.

In the book you will notice S. S. and R. K. at the end of each section. This is to indicate the particular writer of the section, even though the book is a collaborate effort, and both authors stand behind the finished manuscript.

One part of this book draws on a collection of 1464 letters from the public debate about same-sex-partnerships in Norway in 1999 after the re-instatement of Rev. Siri Sunde in the Nordre Land parish in the Diocese of Hamar. The letters provide a window into the writers' *image of God*.

The last chapter of the book contains fifteen *Images of God* that both of us have found to be inspiring and helpful. We do this in the hope that others may find the same. They are meant to be antidotes against god-images that for some reason may have turned out to be toxic.

We begin the book by sharing our individual stories leading us to examine how our God-images came to be.

Susanne Sønderbo and Rosemarie Köhn
October 1, 2003

1

Godpoisoning

THE FIRST TIME I encountered the word "godpoisoning" was in 1976. I was a young novice then, on my way to the convent school in Münster, Germany. I was outside a bookstore and in the window I saw a display of new books. One was titled "Gottesvergiftung" (Godpoisoning), written by the German psychologist Tilmann Moser. I didn't get to read the book until 20 years later, but the title made a strong impression on me. It was a provocative title; a linguistic bomb creating havoc in the regular usage of language. Most people would say this is an oxymoron. When the word *God*—naming the holiest, most sacred—is put together with a negative word *poisoning* there is a conceptual dissonance. This of course was intentional.

Poisoning is a medicinal term. Poison enters the blood stream and rapidly affects the whole body, not just a part of it. To counteract a poison you administer doses of antidote often over a period of time. It may take a long time to recover from poisoning. This is similar to what happens if you have been given a negative and distorted *image of God*. It affects your whole life—thoughts and actions—and it takes time to alter your *image of God*.

Who then are the people suffering from Godpoisoning? Often they are people raised in homes with a single minded Christianity. They have been taught one sided "Bible facts"; that God is to be feared; that God is the judge; that it will be horrible on Judgement Day. These *images of God* have become entrenched in their young and sensitive minds and further strengthened because they were told by people in positions of trust and authority (parents/clergy/teachers). A distorted *image of God* arises when a single aspect or attribute of God is overemphasized or absolutized.

Often people assume that their *image of God* actually is God. What happens then? People become locked into their own (limited) understanding of the nature of God. They do not consider that God may be envisioned in a variety of ways; they simply know what God is like.

Godpoisoning then, is a term used for a religious belief with destructive and disastrous properties. These destructive and disastrous properties are (most often unconsciously) guiding a person's life—rather than a dynamic faith relationship with God. A belief of this kind is particularly destructive when it is long held and rigid—immune to change and development. While we grow in most aspects of life—socially, emotionally, and intellectually—many remain stagnant spiritually/religiously. Stagnation in a negative *image of God* can make life very difficult both for the person and for the people who relate to the person.

Moser's book starts with this sentence: "Dear God. First I have to curse You and scorn You so I can feel relieved." The book is an autobiographical exposition of the Christian faith. Tilmann Moser directly addresses the God that he grew up with as a child: "You remain in me like a poison in my body and I cannot rid myself of it. You still live in me as self-contempt. I was just a child when You infected me with what is like a disease difficult to cure."

Moser's book is the story of a life lived in oppression and self-deprivation, in which God was present as an always watching Big Brother. Moser's background is a form of Christianity (pietistic Lutheranism) in which both scripture and hymnal texts were interpreted literally; in which a God-relationship every day was a fatal "yes" or "no." Everything was interpreted in the light of this belief. As a child you had no choice. Doubt or a hesitation to follow through would alienate his status as a member of the family. Moser tells in the book what it was like to live with this kind of belief and about his struggle for liberation. His book is in a way the means by which he does this; still anyone who is familiar with pietistic Christianity would know how widespread this phenomenon is and that this is much more than one man's story. However it is also a book that confronts the impact of a negative *image of God* in any religion—particularly what falls under the term "fundamentalism."

Long after reading the book I kept wondering about Tilmann Moser. How was he doing? And then one day, now in the age of the internet, I found the answer. I made a search for "Gottesvergiftung" and I found an interview with Tilmann Moser in a German newspaper Deutsche Allgemeine Sonntagsblatt 1998. It was in the "Faith & Therapy" column and the headline read: "A Servant of God" continuing with: "From bitter

Godpoisoning

accusations against Christianity to a new spiritual life. Tilmann Moser, psychoanalyst, has found a new *image of God*." In the interview he explains that the book he then wrote was a young man's attempt to examine the early childhood beliefs that had been so strongly ingrained in him. He never recovered a sweet and innocent childhood faith, just got in touch with his longing for it. The anger and frustration he once felt led to anger towards God. In his own words: "My God became even more cruel and strict than what my parents and the Sunday school teacher had taught me. I had my own poison laboratory and it was stocked with anger and despair. In here, where no one else was allowed to enter, I made the *image of God* even more judgemental and negative."

Moser managed to alter and expand his *image of God*. Calling himself "A Servant of God" in terms of his therapeutic work, he is referring to the serendipitous experiences he encounters in solidarity with his clients. He regards this *Closeness to God* as an antidote against personal and professional arrogance. He also admits to the arrogance he had as he wrote the book in his youth. At the time he thought that his own intellect was sufficient to understand and grasp the nature of God.

For me all this became a great help. With the concept of "Godpoisoning" and further academic research in religious psychology I was well equipped to identify and name that from which many of my religious clients were suffering. Certainly, this was the case during the time I worked as a psychologist and therapist under the auspices of the Danish State Church. Now that I work as a hospital chaplain in Norway the same holds true. Quite often I encounter people who are afraid of dying, because they fear "The Judgement" and "The Punishment" after death. In recent years I have intentionally focused on my own *image of God*. I have become aware that "Godpoisoning" also applies to me. Interestingly enough this was not laid down in early childhood but in my late youth and early adult life. It was an emphasis on "Sacrificing for God" and "The God who demands your all." I had to re-examine my understanding of an "Elitist Christianity," the idea that "the chosen ones" in a "call beyond reproach" were superior to others. "The Narrow Way" is a secluded life in a convent. The committed life of a religious order is a life abstaining from worldly pleasure, including vows of perpetual poverty, obedience and celibacy. This is referred to as "The Evangelical Counsel" as they are rooted in the radical demands Jesus calls the "Narrow Way" in the New Testament. The assertion that you belong to a chosen group of people is instilled in you again and again. "Many are called, but only a few are chosen." The demands of a religious order are very high. And they precede the lifestyle to which you commit. In reality they require a far greater personal and spiritual maturity than anyone at a young age is capable of having. In my case—dressed in full habit and with a veil—when I stopped and saw Moser's book in the bookstore, it was a cry from the subconscious me on a bright sunny day of spring.

For me life in the convent gradually became a burden and I had to find a new way of life. This being the case does not preclude the same for others. Neither does it imply that anyone in a religious order is suffering from "Godpoisoning"! However, any (religious) group that adheres to set standards for its members cannot by so doing help exclude those who are different. The monastic life style is an obvious example. Less obvious is a "fundamentalist" Christianity, found in "independent" churches based on the "True Gospel." It is no coincidence that congregational members from these "Bible-believing" churches often become fiercely vocal and self-assured when others through their studies of Scripture arrive at other point of view than they themselves.

Such fierce and self-assured points of view were clearly intoxicating the debate about same sex partnerships as it was debated in the Church of Norway in the spring of 1999. The Church had its own "Poison Laboratory" and it bubbled over with toxic insults and accusations. The "Biblical" groups particularly disowned the gay and lesbian (Christians) and wanted them excluded from the Church.

James Fowler has done research into religious development along the lines of other developmental psychologists. (Chapter 4 in this book expands on Fowler's research). Fowler points out that a lot of people in their faith development hold on to a conventional faith that is barred personal reflection and experience. The person has not yet questioned his own beliefs or the institutions of faith from which they originated. Loyalty to institutional belief is the norm. However it is important to grow in understanding and to become aware of ones own *image of God*. Perhaps one will discover that the *image of God* is not totally healthy after all. Henri Nouwen priest and author of several popular spiritual books wrote this insight into his own spirituality at age sixty-three shortly before he died. From "The Return of the Prodigal Son"[1]:

---

1. Nouwen Henri J. M., Return of the Prodigal Son, New York: Doubleday, 1992.

Godpoisoning

It dawned on me that even my best theological and spiritual formation had not been able to completely free me from a Father God who remained somewhat threatening and somewhat fearsome. All I had learned about the Father's love had not fully enabled me to let go of an authority above me who had power over me and would use it according to his will. Somehow, God's love for me was limited by my fear of God's power, and it seemed wise to keep a careful distance even though the desire for closeness was immense. I know that I share this experience with countless others. I have seen how the fear of becoming subject to God's revenge and punishment has paralyzed the mental and emotional lives of many people, independently of their age, religion, or life-style. This paralyzing fear of God is one of the great human tragedies.

Just as we develop and grow in the psycho-social realm throughout life, we also owe it to ourselves to pay attention to our faith development. We must use our intellect to critically examine our faith and the faith-propagating authorities/religious institutions. We must push ourselves towards further acceptance and become comfortable with a life of dilemmas, paradoxes and ambiguities. In this way we may one day enter a new era of faith where no one fights *against* another, but fights *for* a brother/sister; having a faith that is busy turning into reality the vision of a better humanity for all, without oppressing those who beg to have a different opinion. Becoming the ones who infuse hope and life is indeed a future oriented leap of faith.

S. S.

2

Image of God

For it is the nature of God to do good for evil. God is our mother as truly as God is our father.

And so in our making, God almighty is our father by nature; and God all wisdom is our mother by nature, along with the love and goodness of the Holy Ghost; and these are all one God, one Lord. Thus we have our being in our Father, God almighty, and in our Mother through mercy we have our reformation and restoration, and our parts are united and all is made perfect man; and by the generosity and gracious gift of the Holy Ghost we are made complete.

We know that our mothers only bring us into the world to suffer and die, but our true mother, Jesus, he who is all love, bears us into joy and eternal life; blessed be he! So he sustains us within himself in love[1].

JULIAN OF NORWICH WROTE these words in the fourteenth century. It dawned on me in the 70s how significant our *image of God* really is. I worked as a hospital chaplain at the time and feminist theology was breaking through as a new approach to our understanding of God. Feminist theology gave warmth and intimacy to the *image of God* and it made it possible for us women to build new incarnational identities. Newly ordained and an inexperienced chaplain at Oslo's General Hospital (Akershus) I was stunned over the number of people struggling with an *image of God* as The Judge; struggling with fear of judgement. This became apparent in that they interpreted their sickness as a punishment for the way they had lived their life. I didn't think this particular *image of God* was still existent. However the image of the judging and punishing God was etched in the core of so many people. In fact I saw my main task as a

---

1. Julian of Norwich, Revelations of Divine Love, Penguin Classics 1998.

chaplain in getting people to rest assured in the belief that God is a merciful God—sometimes helping dying people to adopt this belief; that God covers our past with forgiveness and wraps our future in hope.

As a bishop I have tried to establish the 8th of March as a day of feminist theology. On this day we make a point of addressing God and talking about God specifically in feminine terms. (8th of March is International Women's Day). I have used prayers like: "God, our mother and father, from the depth of our hearts we cry to you . . . ." Nothing else I've done during my time as a bishop has caused more heated reactions. Letter upon letter stated: God is a Father; God is male.

Another point in turn: Visitation. It is an important part of my job. Sometimes public-relation visits to institutions and government agencies. Once I had a tour of a shelter for drug addicts. No formal talk was planned, but from the moment I got there people wanted to talk about God, faith and the church. The actual agenda was replaced by the flood of questions from the residents. As I finally had to leave one of the residents took my hand and quietly said, almost as the ultimate question: "You mean then, that I'm no longer a condemned sinner."

Why are people so reluctant to call God a mother and talk about God in feminine categories? And why is the image of a judgmental God still so widespread? Well, because we in our liturgies, Bible readings, preaching, and entire functioning as a church again and again support just one *image of God*. Through what we say and do in the church we unintentionally convey an *image of God*. If we just use male categories in describing and in addressing God—as "*he*"—then we create a one-sided *image of God* and disregard that all talk about God in fact is imagery. I truly believe this. "God is a father" people wrote in the letters. I would rephrase this and say "God is as a father" just to make it clear that we are using an image. No matter how well we intend to communicate "father" it is no full definition or description of God's nature. "A metaphor conveys an understanding" says Helge Svare in his book "*Life Is a Journey*." "It is defined (the metaphor) as a way of thinking in which we describe or understand one part of reality in the light of another. A metaphor is especially helpful where we fall short of explanations, which is most certainly the case when we talk about God and the essence of God."

In his book Helge Svare raises the one important question: "What happens when a metaphor becomes so dominant that it excludes all other metaphors? In that case we eventually loose sight of the reality which

Image of God

the metaphor was to explain. The metaphor itself becomes the reality for those who use it." To me this explains precisely what has happened in the case of using an *image of God* like father, he, male.

First of all it is necessary in order to be true to a holistic and nuanced *image of God* to describe and refer to, even to address, God also in feminine terms. Secondly it is important to do so for our own sake as we deepen our perception of God. Incarnation theology and feminist theology supplement each other on this point. Identification and identity, experience of self and self esteem are all related to our *image of God*. I'm not aware of any one who has said it better than Dagny Kaul[2]:

> As long as I can remember I have held that man and woman were created in the *image of God* as equal and ought to be regarded as equal in everyday life. Then one day I went to church in the town of Frogner. At that moment—with fresh cut flowers and candles lit on the communion table it was a woman in a white liturgical gown who turned towards us: A woman! It was Sylvi whom I knew quite well from our student years. Then all of a sudden my experience was no longer that of Sylvi standing there rather it was that of a Woman. It was as if the The Divine reached out to me in the image of the feminine. At that point something happened in me. I had a flash of the wonderful experience it is to be a woman. It was as if I too was filled with a sense of divinity just as I had perceived it through my eyes as I saw the white clad person standing in the front. I felt I was in the complete love of God, as a complete female person. This significantly altered my sense of being a woman.

In case we refer to God using one gender only, we consequently reduce the *image of God* and the magnificence of God with a serious diminishing of our own self-worth to follow. Another good reason to examine our *image of God* in the light of gender is that some women cannot identify with God as a man or father; perhaps because of abuse in their own lives or simply because they had a negative relationship to their father. Reference to God in feminine terms is by no means a modern day phenomenon, as I made clear in the beginning of the chapter quoting Julian of Norwich. It is contained in Biblical texts of much older date.

The creation story in Genesis 1 reads (in Hebrew): "And God created humankind in God's own image, in God's own image he created it, male

---

2. Dagny Kaul, *Feministteologi på norsk* (*Feminist Theology in Norway*). Cappelen Akademisk Forlag, 1999.

and female he created them." To me this sounds like the gender duality is part of God's nature; that the nature of God includes a female and a male element. Often in feminist theology the gender question is brushed over by claiming that God is neither male nor female but above gender. To me it is a well supported understanding of the text and a much more intriguing idea that gender duality is in the essence of God. It is to me an affirmation of our sanctity as individuals, male and female alike; and in a very direct way it underscores the equality of the sexes.

I want to get back to what I mentioned earlier that so many people have an *image of God* as the judge and grand inquisitor and why this is so persistent. It may have a psychological explanation. It may reflect the person's own self-esteem. One's self deprecation. One's tendency to sum up one's own life (and the life of others) when one feels overwhelmed by danger and an approaching death. Or it may have a theological explanation. Sunday after Sunday one has listened to how we as people are sinful and lost. Sunday after Sunday one has observed the imagery of the church with pictures of a joyful heaven and a horrible hell.

Through literature these theological images were etched into people's lives e.g. "St Brendan's Regatta on the Open Sea" from the tenth century, "The Tundale Vision" from the twelvth century, and perhaps best known Dante's "Divine Comedy" from the fourteenth century. In Norwegian literature for example "Draumkvedet" (The Dream Poem). All these works of fiction depict the joys of Heaven and the torments of Hell.

Dante has a comprehensive catalogue of sinners who will end up in hell: heretics, blasphemers, gluttons, vandalizers, frauders, sodomites (people who have unnatural sexual relations), and traitors. Their destiny is described in one of the 34 songs about Hell[3]:

> Resounded through the air pierced by no star,
> That e'en I wept at entering. Various tongues,
> Horrible languages, outcries of woe,
> Accents of anger, voices deep and hoarse,
> With hands together smote that swell'd the sounds,
> Made up a tumult, that forever whirls
> Round through that air with solid darkness staine'd,
> Like to the sand that in the whirlwind flies.
> I then, with error yet encompast, cried:

---

3. Dante Alighieri, *The Divine Comedy*, The Colonial Press, New York & London, 1901.

Image of God

> "O master! What is this I hear? What race
> Are these, who seem so overcome with woe?"
> He thus to me: "This miserable fate
> Suffer the wretched souls of those, who lived
> Without or praise or blame, with that ill band
> Of angels mix'd, who nor rebellious proved,
> Nor yet were true to God, but for themselves
> Were only.

Today it is rather obvious that these writings simply were pedagogic tools in coaching people towards morality and decency and not objective descriptions of a physical reality. However during the Middle Ages the imagery caught on and created its own sense of realism. In the Bible there are a number of descriptive terms and images used to describe God and God's future. For our understanding of these passages it is important that we clarify to ourselves what the intent of the Bible is as it makes reference to the future, to heaven and to hell. Is the text primarily poetic, describing reality, or perhaps relaying someone's dream or vision.

The one dimensional picture of God as the father, the man, the judge can be traced back to our understanding of the Bible, to the way we read it and to our perception of the Bible as the *Word of God*. Do we regard the Bible as a collection of words whispered by God into someone's ear, or as a historic document of a certain person's understanding and experience of God coloured by that person's time and place in the world? How do we reconcile these views: that the Bible is *God's Word* and at the same time it is human words. In our Lutheran tradition we maintain that we must have a perspective from which we read the Bible. Martin Luther compares the Bible to a village in which there are narrow streets, broad boulevards, and curved alleys. All of these however lead to the centre of the village where the well is found. "The centre of the Bible," says Martin Luther, "is Jesus Christ. He is our guide as we read. He is our point of reference in a myriad of possibilities. He is the Bible's 'Head and Heart'"

R. K.

3

God-images and God-representation

EVERY PERSON HAS AN *image of God*, a god-concept. This is our experience gained through therapeutic work and counselling in a hospital setting. The *image of God* is often subconscious, but for us as therapeutic professionals it was often obvious what serious consequences this *image of God* had on the person's life.

This chapter will elaborate on the distinction between *God-concept*, *Image of God*, and *God-representation*.

The *God-concept* refers to the person's intellectual frame of mind (hardware) concerning life interpretation. It is shaped by culture and religion. It is manifest in theology, mythology and story telling. The institutionalized religions (e.g. The Church) want to fill the *God-concept* with its own imagery through formal and informal education. The *God-concept* forms the conceptual basis for any formal or informal group concerned with the maintenance and the improvement of the world. The *image of God* is the individual's emotional and experiential content (software) of the *God-concept*. It is a highly complex personal construct created in a dynamic relationship between outside influences and personal experiences. Further it is helpful to use the term *God-representation* in exploring how the *image of God* develops in an individual under the influence of the physical environment, parents (especially the mother), and other people who play a significant role in the child's life. A *God-representation* may be a person or it may be an object and it will take on the propensities of a "trans-substitute"—providing comfort and care, hope and inspiration; on a different level it may also contain negative properties of fear and anxiety.

What you believe is an important factor in a person's development of identity, self esteem and social interaction. The *God-representation* can also be described as the sum of a person's experiences. This makes the focus on *God-representation* all the more significant.

THE *IMAGE OF GOD*—WHERE IT COMES FROM.

The subconscious *image of God* is established very early in a child's life. It is established on the basis of the relationship with parents and other significant people and is reflective of the image we have of them. However its roots go further back; actually they reach back into our parents' subconscious *image of God*.

Although our *image of God* is uniquely personal there are still a number of commonalities. However it is important to keep in mind that the *image of God* is an emotional creation—not primarily an intellectual one—and therefore it will always be there. When a person grows into adulthood the subconscious *image of God* will still be there and may still play a role in a person's daily life. Most often this happens when a person is under stress or enters a crisis situation. Later in chapter three we focus on personal and religious development and on growth in areas in which there has been stagnation.

In his work Sigmund Freud primarily focused on development in early childhood and named it the *genital stage*. His explanation of a person's *god-representation* is linked to the *oedipal complex* and the establishment of a *super-ego*. For him a person's *god-representation* was created through identification with the "Noble Father" of the super-ego and from this the person projects an image for his whole life; an image that becomes the person's God. This theory does not explain every aspect of the *god-representation*, since a child already has significant life experiences before it reaches the *genital stage* in which, according to Freud, the *god-representation* is established.

Later research by psychologist Ane-Maria Rizzuto suggests the child's experience of the mother relationship during the first years is the most significant contributor to the formation of a *god-representation*. Other significant adults such as father figures, grand parents, aunts and uncles, teachers etc. also play a role. Typically one would use "religious" language in describing the relationship between mother and child. For example one may talk about unity of spirit, omnipotence of the mother, and the perfect harmony of the relationship. During the subsequent years the child is bound to experience a breach in the relationship with the parents and others leading to an "exile from Paradise." However the dream never dies. The person's adult life may subconsciously be a search for "the lost Paradise"—a longing for the perfect relationship and the holistic life.

Erik Erikson uses the term "holy" as he describes the basic emotional relationship between mother and child the entire first year after birth. The *image of God* is a strong emotional construct established very early on in a person's life. In general it is during the first six years the *god-representation* is formed based on the child's relationship to the mother, father and to him/her-self. The mother relationship is the most significant contributor to the formation, and at the same time the most complex influence because it is part and parcel of the growth process.

Jonas Gardell a Swedish author writes in his recent book "*About God*"[1]:

> I was raised by my mom in the town of Enebyberg and by Our Father who art in Heaven. I held sacred the name of both as they both knew each other intimately. And God insisted on honouring my mother while she taught me that God was with me always, and would love me no matter what—he would never forsake me.

> It's a mid-May evening. I'm in bed and dozing off. Sitting on my bed my mom touches me gently, then we pray together: "Now I lay me down to sleep . . ." She sings gently: "Children of our Heavenly Father . . . ." You can hear the rain on the new leaves and the drip of the kitchen tap. The curtains let through a bit of the late outside light. The breeze through the open window moves the curtains back and forth. It feels like breathing with comfort and ease.

Ane-Maria Rizzuto's points out how every person has a unique *god-representation*. For us it seems more correct to say that there are unique variations on the same basic themes. One core theme of the *god-representation* is that of a power that demands and monitors you which in turn leads us to believe that a father representation has been significant for the *god-representation*. This is typical of people born in the first half of the previous century. Among younger generations a core theme is one of an "Ever-loving God." This *image of God* perhaps bends towards wishful thinking and is presumably influenced by the mother relationship. Rizzuto advocates for personal life long growth in the area of *god-representation*. She suggests we deliberately grow in self awareness in all areas

---

1. Jonas Gardell, *Om Gud (About God)*. Tiden Norsk Forlag, Oslo 2003.

God-images and God-representation

of our life. We have an *image of God*—even if we are unaware if it. So why not discover and grow to maturity in this area also?

Erik Erikson examines *god-representation* and also "god-relationship" in the light of our human experiences. We have *Spiritual needs*, he claimed; established by a child's need for parents and nurture; even adults have the same needs. *Spiritual needs* then are our ways of ordering life around one's own experience and of making sense of this experience through active participation in the world, lest one should become overwhelmed by it. Erikson paid great attention to this in his psycho-biographical works about Ghandi and Luther.

This book began with a mention of Tilmann Moser confronting and struggling with what he called *'God-poisoning'*. In the interview from 1998 he talks about how difficult it has been for him to de-toxicfy and rid himself of the "Tyrant God" from his childhood. He no longer uses the "Christian" references and terminology. For him it became necessary to develop a new terminology as he was working with clients who their entire life were struggling with thoughts of "sin" and guilt and as a consequence never experienced any self worth. They felt rejected not only by their parents but also by God and the world (cosmos). As a therapist he encourages the person to have conversations with God as a means of becoming more aware of his/her *image of God* and perhaps remedy the negative effect this *image of God* has had on his/her life. In a role-play the client speaks to an empty chair as a representation of God. The client says to "the empty chair" what he needs to say; vents his emotions—expresses his thoughts and feelings. Then he sits in the "empty chair" and responds with what he imagines the answer might be. This continues until the "dialogue" comes to an end.

This form of therapy builds on the inner dialogue all people have and on the polarization between extreme points of view. When the client assumes the "empty chair" one of two reactions happen. Either the "empty chair" enjoys the torment of the client or the "empty chair" is sorry for the way the client feels. The therapist can then use this dialogue to examine the *image of God* with the client.

The role-play and the confrontation dialogue become the mirror for the client who with the help of the therapist may reach a new level of understanding and eventually rid himself of the *image of God* he adopted from his parents, grandparents, the priest or someone else. In place of the old *image of God* a new one arises, dim at first. When a client steps into the role of God and imagines what kind of an answer he would like to hear from God often God becomes mild and loving. Moser saw these emotional moments as defining and formative for the new *image of God*—holy moments, he calls them.

DEMONIC AND DESTRUCTIVE *IMAGES OF GOD*

The German priest and therapist Karl Frielingsdorf has worked with clergy, convent, and laypeople from the Roman Catholic Church for more than 25 years. He has written books in which he candidly tells about the destructive powers of the unconscious *images of God*. He poses the question as to how such dedicated and sincere believers who claim faith in a loving and merciful God actually can experience the opposite in their own lives leaving them ostracised, deprived, even neurotic or suicidal.

Often the stories have a common trend. In early childhood they were exposed to a primarily negative environment in which people who had authority over them were judgmental, punitive, unpredictable, and bullying. Frielingsdorf draws the conclusion that consequently they developed a negative *image of God* based on the negative environment created by parents and other adults. Out of fear of punishment the *image of God* is suppressed and becomes subconscious. Meanwhile for the world to see they take on the image of a religion—Christianity—that talks about God as a loving Father and a good shepherd. Internally they are plagued by guilt, fear and shame. The merciful God is not internalized—not for them!

Destructive *images of God* are very powerful in that they are subconscious. However in Frielingsdorf's experience it is possible through therapeutic work to uncover the negative *images of God*, to discover their origin and even to replace them with positive and edifying ones. This is (at least) the case within the Christian tradition.

A destructive *image of God* arose in the context of a single aspect of God being overemphasized and made absolute. In this fashion God may become a "rule enforcer," "morality keeper" perhaps "God of the Ten Commandments" who demands obedience to rules and does not tolerate any deviance.

Examples:
a. *The Mean Judge*, who accuses as well as executes judgement. Wrongdoing is dealt with harshly and punishment is administered immediately for the sake of law and order and a smooth running society.

b. *The Accountant*, who keeps a record of right and wrong and who eventually will decide a person's life account on the basis of merit.

c. *The Enforcer*, keeping an eye and ear on all that is said and done, that nothing illegal may be tolerated. Fear of punishment keeps you in line!

d. *The Bully*, who holds power over you indiscriminately and does this or that depending on the mood of the moment. This *image of God* clearly reflects a traumatic experience of arbitrary parenting—being dependent on the whims of the parents.

The destructive properties of a person's *image of God* may not be due to a negative religious upbringing. The roots of the negative image may go as deep as the pre-natal stage (before birth). Perhaps the person was an "unwanted" child and the pregnancy was unwanted, inconvenient, or shameful. An emotional transfer may take place so the person will carry this shame in his/her being for the entire life, unless it is dealt with in some direct fashion. A destructive *image of God* is the result of a life experience at a pivotal point of impression in a sensitive person's life, for example the feeling of being "unwanted." "Wrong Sunday School teaching" on the other hand is not the root of a destructive *image of God*. It is the preceding emotional endowment in a person that leads to an *image of God* that then is a reflection of that emotional endowment.

For Frielingsdorf the first step to correcting a distorted *image of God* lies in discovering your own basic biographic emotion. Getting in touch with this preceding emotion is central to the construction of a new and more helpful *image of God*.

A negative *image of God* may loose its power if and when a person realizes how it came to be at a certain point in life. Normally as a person grows up the patterns and emotions of one life stage change and emerge into the next stage. In most of life's spheres maturity and development comes easily and naturally—however it is not uncommon to see people stuck at a very early stage in the sphere of religious development.

It all comes back to how previous generations interpreted and lived their *image of God* and through their lives passed it down to a new generation. They may have been inspired from a source like the Bible but the experiential demonstration of the *image of God* was just an interpretation and an incomplete representation of God. It would be natural at this point to exercise some caution. Why even bother with religion? Why take the risk of transferring a negative *image of God* to the next generation? Better not bother at all. While caution is in order the point is clear that it is not as much religion and religious teaching that may result in a negative *image of God*, rather the *image of God* is a by-product that results from our interaction with others.

The *image of God* was established in our emotions (and thoughts) through interacting with the people who nurtured and fed us. Consequently changes can only take place in a relationship with others. Change may be accompanied by strong reactions or be caused by these e.g. trauma and existential shifts. Remember we are talking about changes in our individual perceptions of God—not an objective outside God. Ana-Maria Rizzuto pointed out that our self perception is related to *the image of God* with which we are endowed. Now the real issue is not God but how our *image of God* works in our life. Is it a positive or negative force in our daily life? Often this becomes evident under stress; when we make a decision or make no decision—we may even at those times be aware of our own functioning. However it is in talking on a deep level with another person that important change may occur. It may be a therapist, a spouse, a close friend, a spiritual person or a pastoral counsellor who may be instrumental in the change. It is when trust develops in the relationship that it becomes so profound. Given the right situation it is possible to have a conversation in which hidden issues may be revealed and new understandings may emerge. Some times the conversation is of such significance that it breaks old emotional patterns and opens up new levels of insight. The unconscious *image of God* and the life that flows from it may elude rational thoughts and cognitive behaviour. Only another person can help discover this. Bringing to consciousness the "hidden" *image of God* opens up the possibility of re-examining it aided by the trusted friend—who has no relationship with the people from whom it originated. Perhaps the *image of God* may be expanded and perhaps a more resourceful approach to life will emerge.

A person's self-image and his/her *image of God* are in a dynamic relationship. The same goes for self-image and the parental relationship. One interacts with the other and neither can stand alone.

Tilmann Moser uses rites and rituals as tools of healing in the recovery from *Godpoisoning*. He separates the ritual from its original religious context and brings it back to an ordinary life event. He says: "When I see a mother holding her infant in her arms I sense a fundamental holiness

God-images and God-representation

in her look, her posture, her emotions. I have studied infant development and I see it as the source of the sacred. I regard theology as a way of describing what happens in early life: a juxtaposition of helplessness, trust, and the need for being noticed."

If in early childhood there is a lack of closeness, insufficient eye and body contact, lack of accept, distrust and suspicion—then, says Moser, there is a likelihood that prayer, music, ritual and ceremony may fill that emotional void. He regards those people fortunate who can relate good human experiences with their *image of God*. A religious experience can be either uplifting or threatening. The words from the benediction: The Lord lift up his face and look upon you" may convey comfort and care—or control. It all depends on the experience of the person who hears the words. What remains is a deep human need to be seen and accepted—blessed.

In our chaplain's conversations at the hospital it is common to be faced with the questions: "Why did this have to happen? What have I done wrong? Why did this happen to me? Am I being punished (by God)?" These questions and the following conversations most often reveal that the person is struggling with an *image of God* that is one sided and negative rather than positive—meaning a *harsh and judging God* rather than a *merciful and loving God*.

When a person is going through a crisis his or her emotions often run wild—the person is overwhelmed—snowed under—and regressing to an earlier stage in life. It is rather common that a person goes back to an *image of God* and to a thought-pattern that was present in early childhood. This happens for people of religious conviction as well as for those who are a-religious. It can be a surprise to faithful believers that they become "childish" in their approach. Likewise people who are sworn atheists experience an *image of God* they thought long gone.

The *image of God* can as we mentioned earlier only change through a relationship with another person. Reading, self-help books, sermons and theological studies doesn't do it. Because the *image of God* is lodged in the person's emotional life over a period of time it may also take a long time before change can occur. Conversations with another person of confidence can facilitate the change in that the emotional content becomes more accessible. Often the feelings associated with the *image of God* are strong and "unacceptable"—anger being the most common. The anger is directed towards "*the one*" whom they thought would keep them safe and secure as long as they did their religious duty (prayed, went to church).

Then when crisis struck and they suffered they were ignored by "*the same one*" in whom they had hoped.

It takes a good while before the struggling person can re-work the emotions to also include a positive *image of God*. From the negative image that was endowed through previous personal experiences now emerged a positive image through love and care present in the person (therapist) at the very moment of crisis. With reference to the Christian tradition the love of God becomes personal, tangible, and existential. However from another standpoint it seems that this is a universal truth clad in (Christian) religious language. An *image of God* that includes Jesus Christ is both religious and non-religious in that the human experience becomes the touch point in the emotional life of the person.

The incarnation (God becoming human) is a central Christian principle that applies in a crisis situation as well as in a community setting through congregational assembly. The notion of an avatar—a *god-representation*—is a parallel in Eastern religions.

From conversations with patients we know the close relationship between existential angst and the *image of God*. We have found these conversations to be absolutely crucial in re-entering life on a positive note after a crisis. People find that life and faith become one and contain a holiness of its own. The burden of a religious baggage may be transformed into a life-giving hope. As people who enter conversations of this nature we ourselves become transfer objects for the *image of God*. Good and bad images alike. An experience of acceptance, comfort and being noticed (helplessness, trust, and the need for being noticed) will ultimately change the person's *image of God*. In this way any conversation about our personal *image of God* may pave the way for a richer more nuanced *image of God* that will make connection between an unconscious and a conscious *image of God*. This in turn may result in a renewed appetite for life with joy and hope for the future.

S. S.

4

Personality Development and Faith Development

As human beings we live and change in our relationships throughout life. Our persona grows out of our interactions with others. Our development is physical, mental, emotional and social. We are always in process. Stagnation is the equivalent of psychological death, becoming entrenched in a routine or perhaps a sign of mental illness. A climate of trust, acceptance and care facilitates development. When we experience this sort of environment we feel loved. To feel loved is a fundamental human need. Love makes us grow and mature—makes us be the best that we can be. To keep this perspective on life is essential as we become nurturers for each other throughout life.

Developmental psychologist Erik Erikson does not talk about development from lower stages to higher stages. Rather he talks about development from one "age" to the next "age." Each "age" has its own merit and its own challenge that has to be resolved in order to progress to the next "age." However, if a challenge is not resolved but instead by-passed or avoided then a certain personal issue remains and will later surface during times of stress and anxiety. At that time the person is set back to the earlier emotional state and may now struggle to overcome the challenge. How we face a challenge in life is often based on how we faced a challenge earlier in life.

Erikson rolls out a comprehensive theory of five ages from childhood to adulthood (infant, toddler, play, school, and youth) as well as three adult ages (early adult (20–32), middle adulthood (32–45), and mature adulthood (45–56)).

At each age he turns the spotlight towards three aspects: *the physical, the psychological and the social*—but he leaves out the important fourth aspect: *the existential/spiritual*. Erikson does not go beyond the 56 year when it comes to personal development. On our own account we propose to add an additional three "senior-ages" along with the spiritual/existential aspects in all of the "ages." This is an expansion of the theory that we have found helpful.

Erikson's life cycle theory is an important basic understanding as we take a closer look at faith development and faith crisis at each age. For our purpose we are especially interested in how the *image of God* and the *god-relationship* are influenced by the way we pass through our developmental challenges. Further it is important to distinguish between age-related challenges and the challenges that arise from life's (traumatic) experiences at any age.

James W Fowler, theologian and psychologist, is one of the most notable writers about faith development. Fowler is strongly influenced by Erikson's thoughts and he builds on them to include the missing aspect of spiritual/existential development. Fowler uses the term "faith" in a general way rather than a specific religious way. Even in a secular world faith is important. "Faith" is used as a description for basic values and beliefs in a person's life—not just institutional religious belief. Many other sub-cultures and humanistic societies are based on common values and offer a belief-system to its adherents. We will in this book mainly focus on faith development in a Christian tradition. This will explain the attention and care with which we try to describe an *image of God* that is both relevant to each stage, and at the same time reflects the complexity of the faith.

In other words there is a close relationship between personality development and faith development. Faith does develop from childhood to adulthood. Changes do take place when it comes to the *image of God* and the *god-relationship* whether people are conscious believers or not. However many people simply abandon their childhood faith and do not develop an age-adequate faith for their adult life.

Research in the field of religious psychology testifies to the formation of an *image of God* within the first year of a child's life; also that this *image of God* is influenced by the social and cultural environment. The father and the mother have a primary role in the child's development of the *image of God* but their role is not exclusive. In general the factors that influence development also apply to the religious development and the *image of God*.

Our entire life is shaped by our childhood experience. The formation of our *image of God*, either good or bad, is no exception. How our *image of God* is formed all depends on how well a person passes through a certain age, smoothly or with obstacles. The *image of God* is further developed in adulthood and again if this happens in a positive environment it leads to a *deep faith*. On the other hand if negative influences are dominant it leads to *religious despair*.

What follows next is a description of each age with the variance of a positive and a negative emotional foundation coupled with the possible outcomes for the *image of God*. This will illustrate the spiritually polarized world in which we find ourselves. The descriptions and the chart that follow are based on the work of Erikson, Fowler and Köster and supplemented with own clinical observations and conclusions.

As we roll out the scenario of human personality development we frequently use the term *"a sense of"* e.g. *A sense of dislike*. Such is a reference to a both conscious and subconscious emotional state. It is at the same time an experience (which the person may describe using introspection) behaviour (which an observer may notice) and a state of being (which may be physically tested and analyzed). All three aspects are important for our understanding.

CHILDHOOD'S FIVE AGES

First Age: Infancy (0–1 year)

The positive experience at this early age is a fundamental trust, or belonging, a sense of being cared for "by good hands." The negative experience is one of being unwanted, disliked, a sense of being abandoned or threatened. A positive *image of God* may take the form of a "look full of favour" or "a mild expression." The infant's experience is one of being in the power of something/someone strong and caring. His or her needs are being met with love and goodwill. The opposite experience would be one of indifference, being in the way, feeling unwanted and at the whim of someone's unpredictable mood.

On the positive side the religious experience of trust results in a sense of well being. "It's good that I'm here!" It gives the infant a sense of the numinous and the awe of existence. There is openness towards "life." On the opposite side of the spectrum a negative religious experience gives rise to a basic distrust in everything. "Am I allowed to live?" And the answer is neither "yes" nor "no" but a burning "I don't know." Any sense of the numinous is absent. Instead there is a cynical fatalism and a felling of looming emptiness.

In other words, what happens during the first months of a person's life has a profound impact on the further development of the individual's personality especially when it comes to the polarity between trust and distrust as it is played out at this age. Fowler is of the opinion that the pre-natal development—in the womb—is even more significant. The foetus, he claims, senses through bodily experiences what kind of world awaits it, whether it is wanted or unwanted. Of course the child has no conscious perception of faith or of God; however these early sensory experiences form the backdrop for a person's belief system. That an infant is seen and valued is of absolute significance. If this does not happen it results in unhealthy bonding and dependency. The earliest images of the mother, with whom the child develops a symbiotic relationship, will for the child later invoke images of perfection, love and fulfillment—or of disappointment, random chance, and perhaps even evil. The infant typically wants to hold on to the 'state of Paradise' by idealizing the mother as being perfect and infallible. If symbiosis with the 'mother-god' persists, it may block further emotional and religious development as it hinders engagement with the real world.

Should the basic trust be missing from the infant's development it will effect both the development of personhood and faith. It will lead to a void in religious and numinous concepts.

> The parental faith, which supports the trust emerging in the newborn, has throughout history sought its institutional safeguard (and, on occasion, found its greatest enemy) in organized religion. Trust born of care is, in fact, the touchstone of the actuality of a given religion. All religions have in common the periodical childlike surrender to a Provider or providers who dispense earthly fortune as well as spiritual health.[1]

An adult who still struggles with an issue of trust versus mistrust may often trace this back to unresolved feelings in infancy.

Second Age: Toddler (1–3 years)

The positive life experience at this age is an emerging autonomy, independence and self-confidence. An amount of self-assertion without the

---

1. Erik Erikson, *Childhood & Society*, 250.

loss of identity (Look at me!). On the negative side it would be a feeling of shame and humiliation: I'm not worthy; I doubt I'll be OK; insecurity. The child develops a co-dependence and feels restricted; not free and confident. A certain type of defence mechanism develops; one that seeks to replace the loss of self esteem with control of others. The positive *image of God* portrays someone in whom you can trust, depend upon and negotiate with; a covenant-god who safeguards your life; a positive authority. The negative *image of God* is one where God is a strict judge, a ruler of law and order, a God who is domineering and who decides everything.

In positive terms this religious experience forms the basis for a God who takes humans seriously and vice versa. Both are important. It creates a feeling of confidence and openness and trust in God. Opposite, a negative experience gives rise to the notion that you have no right to even be who you are; being uncertain about God's approval; a lack of self worth. If a person stagnates in this age it may result in fundamentalism and literal interpretation of scripture, seeing religion as a set of rules and regulations.

In the first age the child's *image of God* is shaped in relationship to primarily the mother. In the second age comes a desire to be in control of the whole world. This goes hand in hand with the development of new vital functions such as standing, walking, and control of the bladder and bowel. The father relationship becomes more important. The child turns to the father as a supportive third person, who helps the child break free from the symbiotic mother-child relationship; by mere presence the father provides the child with a relationship to someone other than the mother. It is at this age the child creates an *image of God* as the almighty, omnipotent father-god; with the idealized father picture in the background. This plays a major role in the formation of the super-ego which becomes a centre for self regulation and accountability.[2] The father picture influences the child's drive towards independence and creative expression. It is the dynamic relationship between child, mother and father that gives rise to the *image of God*.

A religious view dominated by feelings of shame and guilt may have its origin in unresolved issues at this age and it may be carried far into adulthood. Shame is the feeling of being exposed. They can see you; but you are not ready for them to see you. Typically we know shame from

---

2. Dieter Funke, *Im Glauben Erwachsen Warden*, 48.

dreams when we find other people looking at us when we are naked, or caught in a compromised situation e.g. in the bathroom. Shame is also known early in life as a desire to hide your face or "sink into the ground." Actually it is a sort of rage against one self, according to Erikson. The one who is ashamed wants the world to look the other way and not notice that you are "naked." Alternately you wish for yourself to be invisible. This dynamic was used in public discipline (during earlier times) by putting the offender in a pillory (for all to see!) or in at school you might be put in the "corner." Doubt is the twin brother of shame. Adults adhering to a strict religious discipline may have issues of shame. One way to 'handle' shame is by focusing on what is allowed and what is not, and by making sure others follow the law (so they won't see me exposed).

This age is crucial when it comes to the ratio of love versus hate, cooperation versus stubbornness, freedom of self expression versus suppression. From a feeling of self-assertion without the loss of identity comes an enduring sense of goodwill and pride. However the loss of self worth and being under 'administration' results in a lasting propensity for shame and doubt. Children at this age are preoccupied with death. They may be afraid of dying but even more afraid of a parent dying. They learn the word *God* and try to imagine 'God'; but God is in general too abstract for them.

Erikson pointed out the relationship between trust and institutionalized religion. The child has a need for affirmation and for limit setting. This is a reflection of the adult world where there are rights and responsibilities for a public welfare. This is institutionalized in the principle of law and order.

> A sense of rightful dignity and lawful independence on the part of adults around him gives to the child of good will the confident expectation that the kind of autonomy fostered in childhood will not lead to undue doubt or shame in later life.[3]

Third Age: Preschool age (3–5/6)

At this age initiative and creativity are the positive hallmarks. A child is typically interested in competitions and often exhibits risky behaviours. The child seems to have a "drive" towards certain "goals." The danger of

---

3. Erik Erikson, *Childhood & Society*, 254.

this age is that the child will feel inadequate and afraid of trying anything new. This may manifest itself in a sense of guilt over not doing it "right" or an anxiety about "ruining it."

The positive *image of God* is one of companionship along "life's path." "He walks with me and he talks with me" (a phrase from a hymn *In the Garden*). God is experienced as one who welcomes exploration in an active search for improvement. On the negative side the *image of God* may turn into feelings of an almighty critical scrutiny that does not recognize people's worth or uniqueness. God does not tolerate deviation from the norm or standard. God is "the eye" watching and remembering all the mistakes in order to cash in on the "debt" later on.

The developmental task of this age is to build religious images that will portray faith as sufficient and an entity that will always be there to lead and guide. In this way the child can enter life trusting God will always be at the right hand beside him/her. In the Hebrew Scriptures the story of the exodus from Egypt describes this very well. God is the one who accompanies the nation as they walk through the Wilderness on their journey towards the Promised Land. The opposite can also be exemplified by Hebrew Scriptures as the Lawmaker-God who is primarily interested in obedience to the Law. This god is not interested in the people themselves.

Every child at every age displays a vigorous quest for learning and growth. This in turn is a challenge for the adults looking after the child. Hope and responsibility keep child and parent learning together. When it comes to initiative and creativity as in this age this is all the more true. The basis for development is always the same:

> ... a crisis, more or less beset with fumbling and fear, is resolved, in that the child suddenly seems to "grow together" both in his person and in his body. He appears to be "more himself," more loving, relaxed and brighter in his judgement, more activated and activating. He is in free possession of a surplus of energy which permits him to forget failures quickly and to approach what seems desirable (even if it also seems uncertain and even dangerous) with undiminished and more accurate direction. Initiative adds to autonomy the quality of undertaking, planning and 'attacking' a task for the sake of being active and on the move ...[4]

---

4. Erik Erikson, *Childhood & Society*, 255.

Storytelling is important at this age; it gives continuity and adds context to a child's world view. Children at this age love to hear stories and fairy tales and being at the same time open minded and vulnerable they are left with life long impressions.

Through storytelling a child's experience of life may become open towards love, faith and courage—but it may also become frightened and traumatized. Fowler describes how he encountered adults who developed personality disorders due to an exposure at this age to sermons and teachings in which descriptions of the devil's power and omnipresence were told vividly and dramatically. Children pick up on teachings such as 'the fires of Hell awaiting every sinner who has not repented and been born again'. Premature conversion experiences have catapulted children into an 'adult faith' often with a long lasting harmful effect on personality development.

Some religious circles and faith groups have a collective identity in codified behaviours—often based on literal interpretation of Scripture—that are typically established and locked in at this age of faith development.

Fourth Age: School age

In a secure and supported environment the child exhibits industry and capacity for work. They are now able to work on a project together and they can complete a task cooperatively. Children have a sense of being useful; 'they need me' and 'I can handle it'. Negatively a child may feel inferior and inadequate, and may not be able to participate in cooperative activities. It feels useless and dispensable. The child only does what he/she is told to do, assumes no responsibility, and does not want to be personally responsible towards anyone.

The positive *image of God* is one of cooperation between God and humankind. God depends on the human race in a sort of co-dependence with humanity. Negatively God is the absolute ruler and the person is in a totally dependent and subordinate relationship to God. It is a master-slave relationship. God does not need human beings except for God's own benefit.

A positive religious experience gives rise to a sense of usefulness in relationship to God: "I want to be involved, develop a sense of co-responsibility, and take pride in making the world a better place to the glory of God." Opposite a child will in no way feel responsible for the world around him/her. Religion becomes a 'hobby' disassociated from everyday life. A sense of legalism and ritualism becomes the norm.

Starting school means a renewed interest in life. Now fantasy is reserved for play since the laws of cause and effect are discovered. Socially this is a crucial age. Since work may be divided and delegated it is at this stage children discover teamwork and their own unique specialty. Religious faith is contained in the stories and legends of previous generations. Still the child has no concept of faith apart from the stories themselves. A literal understanding is the only understanding possible. The child lives in a mystical literal world with only little self awareness.

Fowler makes reference to a great number of adults who have developed intellectually and found great career paths for themselves (as doctors, engineers etc) but have not developed spiritually and emotionally to the same degree. They remain stuck in literal and authoritarian imagery. By the same token there are religious groups (fundamentalists) who deliberately hold on to this stage of scriptural understanding. They tend to exercise strict control over their members' 'performances' which in theological terms is called work righteousness or a theology of glory.

What is required in order to move on to the next age is an understanding of the dichotomy of the collection of stories. Also that each story requires some reflection in regards to its nature and intent. Along with this comes an appreciation for case specific authority with respect to different parts of reality.

Fifth Age: Adolescence

The positively growing and developing youths acquire a unique personality and a conviction of his/her own social and occupational future. They experience a new identity based on previous roles and skills revised in the light of the inner revolution of thought and body. Negatively they may dis-integrate, fall apart, and loose their identity: who am I? what do I want? what is my role? A great confusion of roles.

A positive *image of God* provides the person with a sense of belonging to a world in which God includes humanity as an equal partner with God self. God respects the individual's rights and autonomy. In the opposite case God is perceived to be the domineering and controlling power that does not yield freedom of development.

The positive religious development results in a mature, 'adult' relationship to others. "I accept how God has been evident in my life." This yields a spiritual identity of faithfulness and loyalty. The other possibility is an all together abandoned God-relationship or a relationship to a God of estrangement and totalitarianism.

The adolescent starts to explore intensely other groups than the family. They begin especially to look at themselves through the eyes of their peers: "What do others think of me?" At the same time they explore their role in the peer group. Separation from parental authority is in full swing. However it is important to establish a new authority that will confirm his/her identity. God may become the 'guarantor' for the youth's identity. The *image of God* established in youth is one who confirms and knows who you are. Symbols become important, although youths have a hard time separating symbol from what they symbolize.

Fowler believes a majority of people remain at this age throughout life. The most difficult task of faith development seems to be between this and the next age. This is the conventional age. Since faith at this age is more group-owned than personally acquired most religious organizations and faith groups operate by this approach. The believer does not ask the tough questions about faith itself neither does he/she question religious authority. Unity is paramount; conflict is bad. The world is often divided into two simple groups: "us" and "them."

THREE AGES OF ADULT LIFE

Sixth Age: Early adulthood (20–32)

This age is positively characterized by the ability to develop an intimate relationship, a balance between closeness and distance. A sense of spontaneity is combined with a heartfelt desire for a partner to feel likewise. Negatively this age may result in isolation, the difference between nearness and distance being blurred and accidental. The person experiences a sense of disintegration and isolation due to either a too strong or too weak identification with another person. Consequently it results in self-absorption or in over-identification. In both cases a loss of self is experienced.

Concerning the *image of God* at this age, God may be the friend who will not exploit nor challenge the human vulnerability, but will be there to see you through it (John 15:15). You are intimate with God, just as Jesus is in his intimate relationship to his *abba* (father) God. Negatively God may be perceived as humanity's counterpart, an unapproachable distant authority. God singles out the individual for God self. A sort of negative 'symbiosis' with God expressed in an overpowering presence. This may give rise to depression and lamentation when God is perceived as absent or in aggressive and intimidating behaviour when feeling reassured—on a crusade.

In the positive religious experience God becomes integrated in all aspects of life. There is a mutual healthy respect and autonomy in the relationship—as in a human relationship—a sense of freedom to love and to be loved divinely/humanly. Negatively experienced the person feels overpowered by God for God's own cause. God controls the relationship by a "cause" and the person becomes isolated from the world. Or perhaps the person's only desire is "God" and by this isolates himself/herself.

Transition into *Individuative-Reflective Faith*[5] is according to Fowler the most difficult of all. Also the most time consuming one. In case a person does not arrive at a personally acquired faith before the age of 40 usually the person remains stuck in a conventional faith. Up to this point you have adhered to other people's authority. Faith was given and adopted un-reflected. Now authority becomes an internal state of resting in your own experience and being, and faith becomes a process of situational reflection. It is a painful process to embark upon self-authority in place of an outside authority. Furthermore you have to re-evaluate your professional and private functionings and relationships.

It is at this age the great tension arises between being an independent individual and being a person belonging to a group. The driving force at this stage in faith development is the ability and desire to reflect and think critically in regards to both ideology and own identity.

Seventh Age: Middle adulthood (32–45)

Generativity is the term coined to describe this age's fruitful concern for creative undertakings: reproduction and passing on something to the next generation. An authentic and unselfish concern for persons and things; a genuine concern for the spiritual and religious values to be passed on in a manner that reflects their very nature. In an unfruitful way this is the age of stagnation and self-absorption. You are preoccupied with your own ideas

---

5. James W. Fowler, *Stages of Faith*, 174 ff.

and interests and you have yourself at the centre of everything. The person is 'haunted' by a sense of going nowhere and the shrinking of one's relationships. The *image of God* that corresponds in positive ways to this stage is one where God has chosen a person and is in partnership with humanity. "I chose you and appointed you go and bear much fruit, the kind of fruit that endures" (John 15:16). Negatively God is experienced as self-sufficient, as one who exclusively is interested in own affairs, as one who is unconcerned with humanity's welfare, an authority who knows everything.

From the platform of a positive religious experience this leads to a wholehearted participation in God's plan and God's will for humanity and the world. Responsibility for what is human and divine in the world is mutually shared. On the other hand a negative *image of God* at this age is characterized by religious self-absorption. The person focuses on his/her own religiosity and has no desire for further growth. In this scenario the person really has nothing to offer to a next generation.

The Conjunctive Stage[6] is the term Fowler applied to this age and numerically not many reach this stage of faith development. People at this stage manage to live with paradoxes and make sense of opposite views, and they are interested in what is unknown and foreign to them. In your own reflected and experiential faith you are able to see schisms and contradictions. For the person who lives a conjunctive faith he/she can see the similarity in what seems to be contradictions, and has learned to live with the paradoxes. Consequently God cannot be described in clear terms. God is immanent and transcendent—God is in the world and also separated from the world. God is almighty and vulnerable. God is the master of human destiny and at the same time a human crucified and dying. It is at this stage possible to perceive, express and keep all these divergences together.

Eighth Age: Mature adulthood (45–56)

With a positive world view a person may experience an ego-integration. You accept your own life story and those who have been participating in it: a new relationship to your parents, exempt from your wish that they might have been different, and you assume responsibility for your life in general. You are in solidarity with others and feel connected to them; you want to contribute to society with love and wisdom. There is a capacity

---

6. James W. Fowler, *Stages of Faith*, 184 ff.

to support a cause or organization and a readiness to stand up for own values. One's identity is now deeply rooted and is reflected in the integrity of ones personality. Not so in all cases. The opposite is characterized by despair, remorse, disgust and fear of death; a stance of disengagement and futility towards life and ones own story, self-flagellation, lack of enthusiasm for a cause, no desire to take responsibility and leadership.

A positive *image of God* looks to God as the ultimate source of life and of one's own life in particular. This gives the person a deep sense of comfort which is manifest in a personal surrender of the total self. It is worthwhile to live in God's care. Negatively God is unapproachable. God rules over humanity and knows best. The person with a positive religious experience exhibits a deeply spiritual interpretation of life; a sort of reconciliation with life itself. You live in an attitude of appreciation and wisdom. With a negative religious experience a person's life experience and knowledge will overshadow the divine. God is out of sight and out of mind. Any religious experience is doubtful.

This age may positively result in an acceptance of one's one and only life, the way it turned out, and that it could not have been any other way. In this way a new appreciation and love for one's parents comes around.

> The lack or loss of this accrued ego integration is signified by fear of death: the one and only life cycle is not accepted as ultimate life. Despair expresses the feeling that the time is now short, too short for an attempt to start another life and to try out alternate roads to integrity. Disgust hides despair, if often only in a form of 'a thousand little disgusts'.[7]

Fowler calls this stage the *Universalizing Faith*[8]. The main characteristic is wholeness. Faith encompasses everything and is total in its devotion. You do not fight against others but for others. You know you are not perfect yourself but you nevertheless stay true to your vision. You strive to implement your vision into reality without using force against those who have a different vision.

With such strong belief and with such strong conviction you may be perceived by others as unpleasant. You are provocative in the eyes of the conventional and you invoke resistance. At the same time there is something undeniably charming and eclectic about you. By your vision and

---

7. Erik Erikson, *Childhood & Society*, 268.
8. James W Fowler, *Stages of Faith*, 199.

lifestyle you become a bearer of hope for others. By just being yourself you create a sense of liberation and harmony in the world in a way that is at the same time threatening and liberating for others.

OLDER PEOPLE'S GOD-IMAGES

Erik Erikson's developmental theory does not go any further. However our experience and observation is that change and development continues well beyond this point. In the case of Fowler he does not apply age to his description of the six faith stages. Therefore in an attempt to bridge the developmental theory and the faith stage theory we propose three additional ages of seniority, inspired by Erikson's first three ages. Thus we round off the developmental theory in a cyclical fashion ending in death: Early seniority (56–67), seniority (67–80), and late seniority (after 80 years). The *image of God* is a central concept connecting the two theories.

Early Seniority (56–67)

A positive approach to life results in industry. You have a desire to pass on your life experience. You are now in possession of insight, wisdom, and knowledge about the human psyche and can easily apply this wealth of experience to any real life situation. It is even possible to learn new "tricks" at a time when this can still be applied to the rest of your life. A negative attitude on the other hand results in feelings of being superfluous; "nobody seems to need the experience I have to offer" and "the younger ones by-pass me" even as "I really want to retire." The *image of God* correspondingly is one in which the person works for God. God provides the harvest. "We are God's fellow workers" (1 Cor. 3). Alternately God is the Exalted Ruler and humans just don't matter.

Seniority (67–80)

At best this is the time where a person may reap the benefit of a life well lived. There is reconciliation with the past and a sense of wholeness—rest on the "laurels." At the worst an individual feels worthless "It would be better if I were not here"; the person's aspiration is not to "bother" anyone, meaning "since I cannot be of use any more." No sense of own worth.

The positive *image of God* is one of God the Redeemer. A negative image of God portrays God as absent or non-existent. Life is a great travesty.

Personality Development and Faith Development

Late Seniority (after 80 years)

The best case perspective is one of a fundamental trust and belonging, just as a child relates in infancy to the loving and caring parents. The circle is complete! Life was good and couldn't have been any better or even different since in your heart you have reconciled with anyone and everything—even the things that could have been. The person has "let go" and is ready to "let God" do the rest. Contrary you may feel abandoned or unwanted. Life is nothing and was nothing. Even the person's own life story is insignificant. Death is the last enemy. Bitterness abounds.

The Good Shepherd is the *image of God* in the first case. The person surrenders gladly into the loving arms of God and like Abraham dies at a "ripe old age." In the other case the *image of God* implies that God is dead. And should God by any chance still be there then God and humans are irrelevant to each other. It's all for naught! Death is the great oblivion.

The three senior ages are significant in that they provide a time for self reflection. The more a person reflects on his/her life the more self-awareness is gained. Not until you understand your own childhood are you able to accept it and experience liberation from the experience.

The past is in the past; it is not possible to change it. However it is possible to reframe the past based on a new understanding of what was helpful and what was not. Perhaps they did the best they could? In the same way reflection may lead to forgiveness of people and "the circumstances of life." Reflection may also lead to a reframing of one's *image of God*. That God was on your side and not against you. Imagine the difference!

"Forgive them for they do not know what they are doing." It is possible that an "accuser God" may actually become a "defender God." It may be a very painful experience to re-live and reflect on the past but it can most certainly produce relief and liberation. A therapeutic process is possible just as sure as certain people have a gift for being therapeutic listeners. Perhaps it will stretch over several years. The culmination of this process is a person's self acceptance. When this happens a person becomes empowered to accept his/her own life story and the people who were part of that story. This will result in a new relationship to parents even after their death; even to accept that they couldn't have done anything but what they did. Also you would experience a new solidarity with other people as they too are in the "same boat." The steps of a transformation of this sort are self acceptance, tolerance, living in touch with your own emotions, wholeness and joy of life. The new *image of God* is one of inter-connectedness and trust in all aspects of life.

COMMENTS AND REFLECTIONS ON THE MODEL OF LIFE-LONG GROWTH

The preceding description of psychosocial and faith development is meant to aid in the understanding and acceptance of human diversity. Our realities are diverse. It is not meant to place people in stereotypical boxes or to belittle anyone. In order to understand and relate to others, perhaps even to be helpful to others, it is vital to have an understanding of the possibilities and the potential for growth in any particular situation.

A diagram is merely a tool for understanding and cannot provide a recipe for action. It is descriptive and shows commonalities and patterns. In each part it shows a scope of conflicts and challenges without implying that all growth takes place at a point of crisis. However Erikson does claim that the psychosocial development proceeds by critical steps—critical being a characteristic of turning points, of moments of decision between progress and regression, integration and retardation[9].

The taxonomy of faith development is not meant as a ladder for upward mobility. It simply does not work like that. It simply provides an overall picture—giving anyone a chance to reflect on own and other people's faith. It is difficult to attach a time frame to faith development, except at the early ages where everything happens so quickly and is linked to physical and psychosocial development.

Fowler does indicate a number of personal and environmental factors that may tip the balance and urge the person to find a new and different way to function as an individual. He points to stress or spiritual unrest as the driving force.

In this case a person may

- use a new way of thinking
- look at "self" in a new way. Experience a change.
- have discovered new reference points (values) and uses these in relating to self and others.
- have found more options for action.

9. Erik Erikson, *Childhood & Society*, 270–71.

Personality Development and Faith Development

Erikson's eight age model has been used as a guide for weeding out the negative influences at a certain age. According to this the first age would produce a total trust and in the second age a full independence. However this is not the intention. Erikson himself stressed that a person living in total trust becomes naive and will not be able to function well in a screwed world. It is equally important to have a measure of distrust. No human being becomes fully independent and autonomous. It is presumptuous to attempt a life without a community or the help of others.

We need to experience both positive and negative aspects of life in order to become trusting and independent people who also know the flip sides of life such as distrust, shame and doubt. This is simply a necessary part of growing up. We must be able to integrate both behavioural experiences in order to live with flexibility and vitality.

Erikson later commented on his age theory that at each age *basic virtues* emerge as the lasting outcome of the favourable ratios mentioned at each psychosocial age:

> Trust versus mistrust: Drive and hope
> Autonomy vs. shame and doubt: Self-control and willpower
> Initiative vs. guilt: Direction and purpose
> Industry vs. inferiority: Method and competence
> Identity vs. role confusion: Devotion and fidelity
> Intimacy vs. isolation: Affiliation and love
> Generativity vs. stagnation: Production and care
> Ego identity vs. despair: Renunciation and wisdom[10]

Faith development entails a series of fundamental changes. From the previous notes you may add how our individual *image of God* will interact with such a change. In certain situations the *image of God* may hinder growth; for instance when the *image of God* is an idealized and controlling "parent" a heavenly God instilling fear and obedience for the person's "own good." Liberation may be hard fought in cases like that.

We have already discussed the crucial role parents play in the development of a person's *image of God*. After Freud's discovery of psychoanalysis and ego-development it became clear that the *image of God* could be a projection of an earthly father; which again turned the focused also on the mother-child relationship for the development of the *image of God*.

---

10. Erik Erikson, *Childhood & Society*, 274.

For some people it creates problems when "father" is used as a term for God. The relationship to the earthly father simply distorts the *image of God*. Most commonly it is because of a strict and condemning or a distant and absent father. Perhaps the father abused the child physically or emotionally. Replacing a father image with a mother image doesn't necessarily change much. Some mothers abuse their children too. Perhaps more commonly it is a symbiotic mother-child relationship that may linger and surface in the disguise of anxiety and fear.

Erikson's epigenetic chart for development throughout life in a series of ages is a framework for understanding, although limited and general. Old age can merely be understood through knowledge of what happened earlier in life. It is a common misunderstanding of Erikson's theory that development is like a stairway where you move from one step to the next. Correctly understood the theory suggests that each critical item of psychosocial strength is systematically related to all others, and that they all depend on the proper development in the proper sequence of each item; also that each item exists in some form before its critical time normally arrives and remains there always. The outcome of one crisis/age determines the way in which the next one is approached.

At the age of 40–50 years most persons reorient the way in which they measure time. While they always measured from the time of birth they start calculating the amount of time remaining. Mid-life ushers in a new frame of reference. That there would be no further development after 56 years of age is unacceptable for everyone. Today the average lifespan has steadily increased in the western world. Death after a long life has become the norm. That in itself is a relatively new phenomenon. This prospect of a long and enjoyable old age is nothing less than a revolution of thought for our generation.

One premise for Erikson's model is life long development and another is that integrity vs. despair in the last age depends on the outcome of all the other crisis ages. Erikson later on modified the theory by adding a ninth age which was actually splitting the last age in adulthood into two: early seniority and late seniority. At least this helps accommodate the growing number of people who live well into the 90s. In psychology the term "elder" is often used from the 60th year and up so we are actually considering a period of life that spans about one third of a lifetime. Should not the developmental theory be further modified to reflect the "baby-boomer" longevity? Keep mature adulthood (45–56) as the eighth adult age but add more senior-year ages after that?

The challenge in the last age of development is according to Erikson the dichotomy of integrity vs. despair. What is at play for the older person is a pull on one side towards feelings of satisfaction over a life fulfilled in contrast to feelings of defeat and disappointment in respect to the youthful ambitions, tasks and ideals one sets out to fulfill. The negative feelings are often reinforced by the aging process itself such as apparent physical decline or disability which may set actual limits to ability, mobility etc. At its best the positive outcome of the conflicting feelings from the reflective process is wisdom. For this to be the case it is assumed that all the previous dichotomies relative to each particular life stage also had a positive outcome. In this fashion integrity becomes the sum of a lifetime of meaning and purpose.

It is on the basis of these thoughts that we propose the additional three ages of seniority. They are in a way a reversal of the first three ages and therefore a return to the starting point in life: the newborn child (infancy). The old person returns to the point of origin. Personality traits and reaction patterns in seniority are based on a replay of early childhood's ages. An older person who feels lonely and bitter likely has a baggage of 'unresolved' processes from childhood and a long life. The cause is rarely the present lack of services or a declining ability. A deeper reflection may often uncover a theme of loneliness that has followed the person since the age of two at which age he/she did not resolve the dichotomy of intimacy vs. isolation which likely was caused by an absence of love and affection from the parents.

In seniority however, it is possible to keep growing. Personal integrity is the main area of growth. It started in the 50s and continues all through life. To grow into this age requires a reconciliation with the past as well as an acceptance of the approaching death. People who reach this point have little fear of death and they have a positive attitude towards their life journey which all result in a state of contentment with the present—even if it is the end of the journey.

A declining physical ability is not necessarily linked to a decline in the ability to learn, think and re-live. Want is often the mother of empowerment. With a genuine desire to embark on new learning the senior can obtain a wealth of wisdom for the rest of his/her life.

> A person does not normally loose individuality with age; on the contrary it is often accentuated. Most basic psychological mechanisms are life long and the need for individual recognition is one of them. As a person grows older so does the liberation from internal and external inhibitions resulting in a more conscious lifestyle. Sometimes this defies social expectations and political correctness and takes on a bold individual expression of freedom and courage.[11]

The last age is the conclusion and culmination. Ideally the person lets go of life as a ripe fruit drops from a tree; or as Abraham who "breathed his last and died in a good old age, an old man and full of years." Recent years' research and experience in palliative care has convinced us that we die in a way that is congruent with the way we live. From the moment we are born and with our reflexes grasp on to a nurse's fingers, life is a series of lessons in "letting go." Suppose we do not practice this along the way in less stressful situations we will not be able to "let go" the day we have to die. From our experience the people who have had a hard time letting go, who have "held on tight," are not the persons who have enjoyed life, rather it is the one who didn't live in a manner he had hoped and who now is caught short of a chance to change it. Anxiety about living has turned into anxiety about dying. Angst about death combined with a negative *image of God* becomes a colossal block in letting go at life's end.

Some seniors tend to become very focused on body functions, especially the declining physical abilities. In their senior years they are pre-occupied with sickness, slow responses and digestive problems. They complain about what they no longer can do and miss seeing what they still can do. This becomes quite a burden for their friends and families.

Others handle this differently. They seem to have adopted a different way of defining health and happiness. Intellectual stimulation, interesting activities, and wholesome relationships are more important to them than immobility and poor digestion. In their value system social and mental wellness is ranked higher then physical wellness. They seem to posses a sort of *body transcendence.*

If you as a senior still regard yourself to be the centre of the universe, it will be extremely difficult to say goodbye to life. Contrast this to an *image of God* in which you are a child of God/ child of the universe and you return to a "parental" love/goodness. This will make for a different exit

---

11. Fossan, & Raaheim, *Eldreårenes psykologi* (*Senior Years Psychology*).

from life. The burial ritual used in the church of Norway says: "From earth you came; to earth you return; from earth you will rise again" ("Earth to earth, ashes to ashes, dust to dust"). In a subtle way this indicates the circle of life and at the same time inspires hope.

In the following chapter we will move from the theoretical description of the *image of God* to an empirical approach. In 1999 the Church of Norway was in an intense conflict regarding same-sex partnerships. Letters were crafted and published as ammunition in the debate, many of them with an expressive *image of God*. Strict and stringent; warm and gentle. Some were lifted from scripture passages; others were gleaned from human experience and the hope of a loving God. Some were based on a literal interpretation of scripture. Some were bordering on disrespect for others; some were hinting an underlying mental illness. It really is incredible how human beings can look at the same-sex phenomenon in such different ways. It points more to developmental differences in faith and personality than to theological differences.

S. S.

BASIC ATTITUDE: FIVE AGES OF CHILDHOOD	
POSITIVE	NEGATIVE
Infancy (0–1 years): - basic trust, homeostasis, comfort - being wanted and accepted - "in good hands"	- distrust - disappointment, abandonment - threatened - unwanted
Toddler (1–3 years) - autonomy - original - independence - self-assured, "stand on his own feet" without loosing identity	- shame; "shouldn't do or be like that" - insecure; a sense of being restricted - co-dependency - submissive to control and loosing identity
Preschool (3–5/6 years) - taking initiative - busy exploring; - creativity and trust in own ability - competitive and willing to risk loosing - inner direction	- guilt; a sense of doing the "wrong thing" - fear of failure - hesitant - feeling of inferiority
School age - industry - competent productivity - cooperative; enjoys team work - mastering life; "I am usefull," "someone needs me"	- inferiority - not willing to work with others around a common task - subordinate; only acts on direct request - shuns responsibility; declines care for others' well being.
Adolescence - identity; trust in own ability and worth - ideology; abstract thinking, values and ethics - trust in own personhood and social development - conviction about vocation and sexuality	- loss of identity - role confusion - doubt about what "will happen to me" - following a strong leader

Personality Development and Faith Development

IMAGE OF GOD: FIVE AGES OF CHILDHOOD	
POSITIVE	NEGATIVE
Infancy (0–1 years): - God experience as "a smiling face" - good care and control - to be looked after - goodwill	- God is anonymous; like someone behind frosted glass, - an indiscriminate power
Toddler (1–3 years) - God grants a safe environment - God as the positive authority	- God as the judge; the one who upholds "law and order" - a domineering God who decides everything
Preschool (3–5/6 years) - God as a companion on the road - a God who allows play and exploring; - a God who allows variety and creativity of expression	- a God who watches to find deviance and fault; sees and hates what is "wrong" - critical and posing a threat - overpowering
School age - a God who wants people as co-workers and who need help in finishing creation which is the salvation of all. - mutual dependence; God as "one of us."	- God as an absolute ruler; humans are nothing without God - Humans are God's slaves - God is God—and humans are nothing
Adolescence - a God who identifies with the human experience. - a God who respects human diversity and who accepts the various manifestations of faith, hope and love.	- a God who has "my way or the highway." - demands surrender of freedom and individuality; conformity

BASIC ATTITUDE: THREE AGES OF ADULTHOOD		*IMAGE OF GOD*: THREE AGES OF ADULTHOOD	
POSITIVE	NEGATIVE	POSITIVE	NEGATIVE
Early Adulthood (20–32 years) - capacity for intimacy; an ability to be close and apart - spontaneity - heartfelt relationship that allows freedom	- blurring of boundaries - isolation as a result of over identification - self-absorption - cocooning	- God as a friend - a God who respects and upholds integrity - a God who is a confidante (balance between closeness and distance)	- God possess the individual. - God singles out the individual for God's own purpose.
Middle Adulthood (32–45 years) - generosity - generativity; creative productivity - to pass on life to a new generation - authenticity - care for creation - passing on of values without demanding conformity	- stagnation - self-absorption; exclusive interest in own affairs and ideas - feeling of estrangement from society and friends	- God who chose humanity "to go and bear much fruit, the kind of fruit that endures" (John 15:16)" - God is an eclectic partner for life	- God is known as self-sufficiency. - God cares not about human happiness only about obedience to God's will.
Mature adulthood (45–56) - ego integration; accept of own life story and the people who participated in it - new relationship to parents - solidarity - contribution to the world with love and care - ready to champion own choices for the sake of humanity	- despair and disillusionment - fear of death - self deprecation and sarcasm - lack of enthusiasm and will to stand up for a cause and in defence of others.	- God as the source of everything; foundation for all being(s)	- God as beyond approach and beyond reason. - God who knows it all and keeps it hidden in mystery.

Personality Development and Faith Development

BASIC ATTITUDE: THREE AGES OF SENIORITY		*IMAGE OF GOD*: THREE AGES OF SENIORITY	
POSITIVE	NEGATIVE	POSITIVE	NEGATIVE
Early Seniority (56–67 years) - industry. - a desire to pass on your life experience. - insight, wisdom, and knowledge about the human psyche - desire to learn new ways of living.	- feeling of being superfluous; - "nobody seems to need the experience I have to offer"	- the person works for God. God provides the harvest. "We are God's fellow workers" (1 Cor. 3).	- God is the Exalted Ruler and humans just don't matter.
Seniority (67–80). - feelings of a life well lived. - reconciliation with the past and a sense of wholeness - rest on the "laurels."	- the individual feels worthless - "It would be better if I were not here"; - the person's aspiration is not to "bother" anyone, - no sense of own worth	- God the Redeemer	- God as absent or non-existent. - life is a great travesty.
Mature seniority (80–100) - fundamental trust and belonging, just as a child relates in infancy to the loving and caring parents. - the circle is complete—accept of your life the way it was - have reconciled with anyone and everything - the person has "let go" and is ready when death will happen.	- feeling abandoned or unwanted. - life is nothing and was nothing. Even the person's own life story is insignificant. - fear of death where once there was fear of life - bitterness abounds.	- God is The Good Shepherd - the person surrenders into the loving arms of God and like Abraham dies at a "ripe old age."	- God is dead. And should God by any chance still be there then God and humans are irrelevant to each other. - It's all for naught! Death is the great oblivion.

5

The *Image of God* and the Debate over Same-sex Partnership

WHILE WE WERE ENGAGED in our work on positive and negative *images of God*, Godpoisoning, and the formation of *God images* it occurred to us that it would be interesting to go through the large volume of letters addressed to Rosemarie Köhn during the winter and spring of 1999. Rosemarie Köhn being the bishop of Hamar, Norway was flooded with letters as she proceeded to re-install Siri Sunde in a parish after she openly had declared herself in a same sex-relationship.

Would this source of 1464 letters reveal anything about *God images*? In order to leave out the subject matter we screened the letters with this in mind: What is the pain issue in the negative reaction? What is the cause for joy in the positive reaction? Why did some people react to the decision to reinstall Siri Sunde with joy while others reacted with pain? Are there certain *God images* embedded in the letters?

As mentioned 1464 letters were put into archives. However about one hundred letters sent to the bishop's office at first were shredded after they were read. They were mostly negative. Soon though, the bishop's secretary started to file the letters. She realized that perhaps the letters would be of interest later on. The amount of positive letters is astounding: 1358 letters, a collection of 3598 signatures in support, and 92 bouquets or flower arrangements with a card. The negative ones amount to 106 letters, a collection of 174 signatures in opposition, and no flowers. Even when we include the first batch of negative letters that was destroyed, it is remarkable how few negative letters were received in comparison to the number of positive ones. In the public debate on the other hand negative reactions were very prominent: in newspapers (articles and letters to the editor), radio, and TV. The newspaper clippings were archived by the

The Image of God *and the Debate over Same-sex Partnership*

bishop's secretary as well and they fill several volumes of scrapbooks. This publicly printed material is not included in our analysis. Even though we do not subject our study to statistical analysis, there was an almost even balance between the number of male and female letter writers. The negative letters are for the most part written by seniors and older adults. This is evident by looking at the handwriting and by the style of language and often the person reveals both age and marital status. The positive letter category represents a much broader age group; from 14 and upwards. It also contains letters from older people who express relief that things have changed since they were young. An older woman who was raised in a "prayer assembly" wrote: "Jesus' love was only for the ones in the prayer assembly. Everything and everybody else was condemned."

As I mentioned, we want to focus our attention on *pain issues* and *joy factors* in the letters. We have selected an equal number of quotes from each category in order to demonstrate the depth and width in regards to the *image of God* expressed directly or indirectly in the letters.

NEGATIVE REACTIONS

From the negative letters we have selected the following 18 quotes in random order.

- You are totally blind, without insight, and the personification of Anti-Christ.
- In the eyes of pagans and the blind you are a popular person, but for us who fight for God Jahveh's cause, you are an Anti-Christ and a scum. (The letter is signed by a person who self declares to be a "Bible teacher and master theologian in Southern Norway"
- You in the Church reject God's true word.
- It is not hard to see that the time for Jesus' return is approaching. The signs are right before our eyes. The Church in Rome decayed from the inside and out. Likewise it is with the Church of Norway. It is rotten to the bone and beyond. It is The Great Harlot. Homosexuals are the lowest levels of humanity. Lowest of the low.
- The Church of Norway has become a Harlot-church. (see Rev 18:4)
- You (the four Norwegian bishops) have caused God's wrath upon our country and people—you must wake up before it is too late.

- The Church of Norway is about to disintegrate.
- Might the state of affairs in Norway be comparable to that of Nineveh?
- You are a nice lady, but how tragic that you are lured by Satan to destroy people and betray God's word (Rom 1:18–23).
- It is not right to re-write and alter the only true word of the Bible,—it is down right dangerous.
- "Go and sin no more."
- Have you accepted Jesus Christ as your Lord and Saviour? Maybe then you would read the Bible in a different light.
- Be not so arrogant that you try to twist God's word to fit your own view of things and issues. Pray to receive the Holy Spirit and become obedient to God's word and command.
- If God's word no longer may judge and put the spotlight on our sins, then also grace is irrelevant. What is there to be saved from if there is no sin? In this case we knock out the bottom of our entire Christian faith. In principal the Christian Faith is precisely the infinite grace for fallen sinners who realize their wrongdoings and the need for God's mercy.
- Christian love is to make people realize that they are sinners, that they need God's grace, and that only the blood of Jesus can save them from eternal death.
- Do not change the established boundaries.
- There is so much despair and frustration over this (same-sex partnership), and it is so because it is intertwined: the Devil's tactics inside the Church (which should be God's house). The powers from the abyss are mighty loud and subversive.
- I am baptized and confirmed and for a while I figured that this would be the ticket to heaven; fortunately we have pastors from a previous era who have told us that the road is to receive salvation and learn to live and grow in grace and to work for our salvation with fear and trembling.

Below you will find four letters, three of them in their entirety.

Letter #1:

The Image of God *and the Debate over Same-sex Partnership*

Bishop Rosemarie Köhn,

In my Bible it says that the men turned away from the natural use of women and used men instead, and that this was disgusting in the eyes of God!! It is an equally great disgust today, because Jesus said: Heaven and earth shall pass away, but my words shall not pass away ever. Pastor and bishop alike are to preach the word of God clearly and purely, and not to accept and bless what is obviously against the Bible. If you go against it you have nothing left to tell people who come to church to listen to the word of God, which is what you should preach, instead of preaching and accepting licentiousness! Jesus said to the sinful woman: Neither do I condemn you. Go and sin no more! But you say, "Carry on; you have the church's blessing"! Nostradamus predicted that the clergy would receive its punishment, and I am starting to understand now. It also says that everyone whose name is not in the book of life will be thrown into the Lake of Fire; these are clearly the words of the Bible!

[Letter written by an older woman]

Letter #2:

To Bishop Köhn!

What a horrible person you are, daring to change God's law about sin. It is a judgement on the Church of Norway that people such as you four bishops should lead the congregations. How dare you misguide so many people? Everything we learned and believed from we were small is torn to pieces.

It suits the so called "world" to have opinions like that to guide them. Quite disgusting; and hopefully you will reap from your actions; what would Jesus say to this? Have you thought about this? You are disrespectful and belligerent with your whole being. One who bemoans the development of our church. Sincerely hope that people will wake up and see the danger behind such Anti-Christian initiatives.

I do hope you wake up and see the severity in that for which you likely will get secular applause. It is bad enough with homosexuality and the like, but what are they doing in the church as preachers?

Shameful to the worst degree. Could easily have supplied name and address, but feels it serves no purpose. Hope I am spared seeing your face again on TV. Just getting sick of all this new stuff. Do you really believe God accepts this?!

[The letter is anonymous]

Letter #3: The following is a P.S. (Post scripted footnote) after a long letter

P. S. Haven't sent the letter yet and feel like I have to add a few words.

Gay and lesbians are totally in opposition to God's word. And they are under judgement—unless they sincerely turn around and pray to the Heavenly God for mercy and strength to get out of their situation. A prayer I'm sure would be heard and answered. The Lord Jesus Christ came to save and to free us for living a new life.

Judgement is at the door, now, in Norway too. The Labour Party (Arbejderpartiet) is advancing un-godly legislation—one worse than the other. Catechism to be banned from schools and the rest of society. Islam and other religions advancing. Likewise Roman Catholicism with the pope leading the way. This is God's judgement on our country and people and it is caused by the preaching of a gospel that allows a life in sin against God. Repentance means living a life different than before. A person who does not adhere to this in her preaching ought not to preach God's word. The judgement should firstly affect God's house. You have a big responsibility—and at the same time a chance to preach as John the Baptizer did when he was sent to prepare an obedient people for the Lord.

There will likely be a cost to telling the truth today also, but it is better than being thrown somewhere where worms never die and where fire is not extinguished.

Use the chance you have—be a trumpet in an age of confusion when nobody knows what is right or wrong. Or don't you know?!!

Please be wise and take my letter seriously. I am greatly disturbed about our era. Think about all the violence. When the light is rejected darkness is upon us and the acts of darkness. Jesus says: "When the light in you is darkness—how great, then, is the darkness."

God bless you to be vigilant!

[Letter from an older woman]

Letter #4:

On behalf of myself, my children, my grandchildren and the majority of the Norwegian people—I cannot help but warn you very very sincerely—one more time.

This blood dripping dissention for which you and the three other bishops are the spokespersons—is so outrageous that I feel like throwing up. God never, never, never created a homosexual; it is an illusion

The Image of God *and the Debate over Same-sex Partnership*

from the abyss that captures especially our youth in our time. The Bible is CRYSTAL CLEAR: *"The one who practices this, in which not even the animals engage will be eternally lost.* God cannot fail God's own word so the judgement stands firm."

It is the one who warns others about this and other sins—who has love and care for others.

You are not allowed to bless people into eternal damnation. You cause God's wrath upon our country and people—YOU MUST WAKE UP BEFORE IT IS TOO LATE.

When I read the Bible for the first time about 50 years ago—I could not in my wildest dreams have imagined that there would ever in human history be any debate, dissent or difference of opinion about this matter.????? One almost has to look in the mirror—to check if one really is alive or one is lying in the desert witnessing a mirage. It is so unpleasant one suffers and cries night and day. The support you have is from people who seldom or never have opened their Bible—and who are happy to continue living in their sins. If you cared about the homosexuals—then you would have warned them early and late, instead you given them your blessing even though you know the Bible says that such cannot inherit the kingdom of God. What an unpleasant responsibility that rests upon you. We are scared for our life that our grandchildren should listen to you on the TV screen. You do not know what kind of suffering you bring upon us parents and grandparents.

You openly preach *the worst kind of filth and perversion that has occurred in human history. Luther would not even mention this filth by name.* With the kind of preaching you deliver one may as well put away the Bible—rubber stamp, preach, and give a green light for any possible filthy endeavour.

If same sex partnership should not be touted as sin—then all kinds of ugliness is sanctioned. Preachers may as well pack it in and find other jobs. No, Rosemarie Köhn—YOU ARE ON A WAYWARD TRACK AND YOU LEAD PEOPLE ASTRAY.

[Letter signed with name and address from a man about 70 years of age; the highlights in the text are done by the man]

POSITIVE REACTIONS

Following in random order are 18 quotes that are typical positive reactions.

- You give the Church a human face.
- A Church that is inclusive—not exclusive.
- You demonstrate that Jesus' love includes all people.
- You defend the vulnerable and put love first; you show compassion, tolerance, justice and neighbourliness, reconciliation, vision and courage.
- Many of us feel that the ceiling of the church has become transparent so that you actually may catch a glimpse of the universe in which love and personal worth are central.
- Your view of humanity inspires hope for many
- You communicate the greatest and most important in our church— a transcendent love; you show God's hospitality and generosity.
- Your decision implies that many who thought about leaving the state church actually will stay.
- You give meaning to the concept of a "Church for the People," and you have opened the church for people who feel alienated.
- You have in a way prevented several suicides.
- There is room for everyone in God's realm. We also believe your actions will bring more people to the Church.
- You have taken one giant step towards a more open, inclusive, forgiving and understanding church.
- You exemplify an *image of God* and a view of humanity that ring familiar and hopeful for many in our church today.
- You open a door to the church that was about to be closed.
- Jesus condemned nobody, and he was a rebel in his time.
- You have made a quantum leap into a new era; and you have done it in the name of heavenly love.
- Because of you the church will have less to apologize for in the future.

The Image of God *and the Debate over Same-sex Partnership*

- I am neither a church member, a Christian nor lesbian, but you give me a positive impression of Christianity. The idea that the Church is roomy; and I am proud of being a woman of your time.

Four letters from this category.

Letter #1. It was also printed in the magazine "The Diaconal Home." An open letter to a bishop.

Dear Bishop Rosemarie Köhn,

First I would like to congratulate you and thank you for the stand you have taken in the Siri Sunde case.

I have decided to write to you even though I have no particular interest in this case. I am a "heterosexual atheist," and I have for many years practised psychiatry in the public health care system and become experienced in working with people who for various reasons have problems with self and society. I have so often lamented what I not primarily experience as a lack of love from society or individuals, but rather an incredible lack of knowledge that may be disguised under many forms and names.

As a psychiatrist I have worked with people in crisis triggered by other peoples' misinformation causing severe identity confusion and ethical ambiguity. I often felt like screaming: It is not so; anyone should know this.

I am convinced that you by the stand you have taken are doing more for a lot of people's mental health, self esteem, and liberty, than a hundred "Rainbow-Days" or "Mental Health Days." Instead of emphasizing diversity, minority rights and difference of lifestyle, you have demonstrated equality, dignity, and inclusivity. I believe it means far more than you are aware of today even though you already have been praised and celebrated by some and flogged by others.

When I, for whom this case is impersonal, felt touched and glad when I saw you on TV at the crunch time in January and February, I can just imagine the effect this would have on people who are personally involved, both inside and outside the Church.

It was my impression when I saw you on TV that the process has taken its toll on you. You appear as a person of great personal integrity and humility which I also believe you are and as an atheist I actually have the deepest respect for one who through prayer and/or meditation manages to arrive at a stand that is contrary to the majority and the conventional dogma. How much in our history might have been different if more had had this courage? And how else is progress taking place if not by using disagreement dynamically?

This brief greeting is sent in the hope that you may have the strength to continue for many years as a bishop, and should I one day find a faith may it be through this kind of demonstration of the gospel of love that you have exemplified.

Heartfelt and warm greetings from
Torgeir Husby

Letter #2.

Dear Rosemarie Köhn,

I want to thank you for your reinstallation of Siri Sunde and for your articulated stand regarding people in appointed offices. You come to represent a view of human nature inside the Church that inspires hope for the *church of tomorrow*, one that in my opinion is the only possible approach coherent with *a loving God*.

Thanks for your courage!
Sincerely
[Letter from a woman identifying herself]

Letter #3.

Dear Rosemarie,

In an age where "dog eats dog" I wish to express my admiration for you and for the way in which you demonstrate your respect for others.

I am not particularly religious and have only little affiliation with homosexuality, but what we need more than anything today is charity and that we do accept each other the way we are with our faults and blemishes, good as well as bad.

Neither am I a clairvoyant but I do declare that when history is written a hundred years or so from now, then you will be towering like a lighthouse of the Church as an example of what Christianity should be like—*kindness towards your neighbour, reflective and grace filled living*.

You should never doubt that you have a broad backing in the Norwegian population at a time like this which must be difficult for you. There are many who admire you.

Kind regards
[Letter from a man identifying himself]

Letter #4.

Dear Bishop!

I feel a need for thanking you in this way for the historic, good, wise and courageous decision.

Remember when you feel low that a great majority of the Norwegian people have the same opinion, if this might mean anything to you. Perhaps it may also be helpful that our more recent church history contains an abundance of examples of how similar courageous acts have moved us forward and upward and subsequently resulted in a not insignificant amount of embarrassment for the opponents.

It is mind boggling for many that there are church leaders who seriously doubt what The Master would do had he been walking the earth today. For many of us it is also thought provoking that darkness, the joy- and loveless seem to be concentrated in certain geographical districts and regions of our country. We are proud of you, and in my imagination I dimly see how the Lord smiles and nods—he too is proud.

We are many who pray about strength for you at this time. Carry on with our support. With the best of greetings.

[Letter from a man identifying himself]

REFLECTIONS ON THE LETTER WRITING CAMPAIGN

It was a lot of letters to read through, and a lot of them were powerful and disturbing. The letter reading had to be broken up into smaller portions, otherwise it was too much. It wouldn't be fair to say that all the letters directly are about the *image of God*. Most of them are about the use of the Bible, about human nature, about the nature of the Church, or about love.

When we look at the negative letters most of them declare that Rosemarie Köhn has failed to follow God's word, abandoned God's true word. Her view of homosexuality and partnership is labelled as sin, something that is under God's judgement. Gays and lesbians who practice their sexuality are described as sinners and people who are lost; they are the "scum" of humanity.

Behind the negative letters there is most often (but not always) a so called literal interpretation of the Bible. They do not accept the Bible as a product of the time in which it was written and thus reflecting popular thinking and values of that time. Some letter writers in the negative category are not "fundamentalists"—literal readers of the Bible; however they still declare homosexual practice to be against God's word. These letters express a great amount of pain over the different interpretations of the relevant passages in the Bible, and a different way of using the Bible. But what is perhaps the most significant revelation in the negative section of the letters is a striking aggressiveness; and one can only wonder why.

Looking at the positive letters most of them mention that Rosemarie Köhn shows human kindness, puts a human face on the church. This human kindness is often traced back to Jesus. By having access to any job within the church the homosexuals are given back their true human worth.

The people writing the positive letters stand apart from the literal interpretation of the Bible, and some of them use Jesus and his love as a reference. What is at the centre is Jesus way of relating to people as an expression of God's unlimited love. The joy expressed in these letters is over the humane attitude that literally opens the church's doors for people of homosexual inclination, a group that has been excluded throughout most of the Church's history.

From a neutral point of view it is perhaps obvious that behind the bulk of the positive letters there is no expressed use of the Bible, rather it is a heartfelt humanist attitude. Generally speaking it is astonishing how the "Siri Sunde case" virtually engaged the entire population, and again you are left wondering why.

Two distinct camps can be identified from the letters. One group starts with a certain view of the Bible and a certain *image of God* and from this arrives at a certain view of humanity and of homosexuals. It is most often negative, but not always. The other group starts with a positive view of humanity, a view that includes homosexuals, and a kind of simple trust in God's love; in other words a positive *image of God*.

Entrenched in many of the letters is an *image of God* either as the God of judgement or as the God of mercy. When people experience the church lashing out, then they experience God lashing out also. What effects do these *images of God* actually have on us? There are lots of indications that those who in this collection of letters have a judgmental *image of God* perceive themselves to be truth tellers to a mild or extreme degree. The *image of God* gives them the drive and authority to speak on behalf of God. Some do it reflectively, while others let it all out unreflected. We notice that the *image of God* and the view of human nature are closely related.

The Image of God *and the Debate over Same-sex Partnership*

The pain inducing factor in the letters is quite obviously the use of Scripture, while the cause for joy may be found in the concept of humaneness, which perhaps also might be traced back to Scripture.

We notice in general that many strong emotions are expressed, from "I feel nauseated, I feel like throwing up, I get sick to my stomach" to feeling words like "joy," "tears of joy" "pride," and "When I heard on the car radio that you had reinstalled Siri Sunde I became so emotional and happy that I had to pull over in a parking lot to allow myself a good cry of joy and relief. I'm not even homosexual, but I felt the joy and the liberation on their behalf."

There is a lot of anger in the negative letters, mixed with an underlying fear. And lots of joy, relief and gratitude in the positive letters. It is also remarkable—after the often referred to live TV-debate—how those who were positively inclined have expressed how Rosemarie Köhn "was luminous, almost shining and radiated peace and human warmth." The negatively inclined thought she looked "ominous," some became "sick" just by looking at her on TV. This speaks to the person's preconceived idea. You see what you want to see. But these strong emotional expressions seem quite out of coherence with the letter writer's age, social status, and the atmosphere in which they appear to have grown up. It almost appears as if nature gave way to nurture. Is it bottled up anger that comes to the surface, or is it perhaps rather a sign of emotional immaturity?

In the negative letters we also noticed that many are preoccupied with God's judgement on those who live in a same sex partnership: "Nostradamus predicted that the clergy would receive their punishment, and I am starting to understand now. It also says that everyone whose name is not in the book of life will be thrown into the Lake of Fire; these are clearly the words of the Bible!" (Letter written by an older woman)

In the letters of encouragement people are more occupied with "the elevated ceiling in the church," an incarnate church that shows God's inclusiveness and ambiance.

We were puzzled by the striking aggressiveness in some of the letters. Aggression is positive or negative depending of the situation. It may be expressed in an active and dynamic participation or perhaps in pettiness and pedantic nitpicking. Interest in religious matters may be genuine and heartfelt; it may also take the form of hypocrisy and saintliness or an obsessive 'crusade' for "God's cause."

The word *aggression* comes from the Latin *aggredior* which means to attack; 'a forceful action or procedure when intended to dominate or master' or 'hostile, injurious, or destructive behaviour or outlook especially when caused by frustration'. In many Christian circles aggression is viewed negatively since it does not match a pious ideal of gentleness and non-violence. This overlooks that aggression can be either positive or negative. In its negative form aggression is greatly undesirable: extreme criticism, resentment, outrage, destructive bitterness, hate and irony, sarcasm and vicious comments behind the person's back. Perhaps these may be inborn character traits; you may be born with a criticizing 'gene'. However it is more likely that it is due to the phenomenon known as *suppression*; since the ideal is gentleness and non-violence the person is afraid of displaying his true feelings. The environment does not allow you to express any form of aggression. This is often the result of an authoritarian home environment.

What we suppress, though, is not gone for good. It surfaces at times in a variety of forms. It may be projected on to others. Aggression deprived individuals may become over-obliged, sugar-coated kind, over accommodating. They want to appear as being of great service, while they are atoning for an (in their own eyes) unacceptable aggression. This kind of behaviour is often a result of damage to the person's fundamental trust in earliest life (Erikson's first stage). Some have a healthy scepticism throughout life while others throw themselves into the arms of a strong authority and by so doing hide their own insecurity and anxiety.

From my background in psychology I am aware of a variety of motivating factors behind people's actions. My hunch is that this is not just about interpretation of Scripture. Possibly it is also about prejudice. In our mind we create *images of adversaries* in regards to people who are different from what we are used to and whom we perceive a challenge or threat to our values. Often a huge gap of knowledge intensifies the adversarial feelings. In a way this is a mechanism of self-preservation and we tend to pre judge (prejudice). In reality this means we judge them before adequate knowledge is accumulated. In most cases it is fear that hinders us in identifying with another person's circumstances and experiences, as Anders Frostenson writes in his poem:

> And still there are walls between us,
> and with chains we give each other restrictions.

The Image of God *and the Debate over Same-sex Partnership*

> Our prison walls are stones of fear,
> the fabric of our convict-clothes is our own convictions.[1]

Fear's defence is to "hunker down," "stonewall" the attacker and not let thoughts, impressions, and ideas either in or out. This is similar to a suppression. Further to this we often unreflectedly order our life by creating categories (of people): *Them and Us.*

Breaking down homophobia's prison walls, built of our stones of fear, is an exercise in patience and it requires a conscience-raising about the psychological defence mechanisms that are at play when we encounter that which at first seems to threaten our identity and inner peace. The person who is insightful and lives in reflective self-awareness has a lot less difficulty relating to people of different traditions and lifestyles. As old *images of adversaries* are about to be dissolved/destroyed it is indeed both frustrating and bothersome for those who have been comfortable and content with having "scapegoats and outsiders."

The situation now concerning same sex partnerships resembles the situation years back when a number of pastors were against divorce and re-marriage (and also refused to conduct wedding ceremonies for them) until they themselves were divorced and re-married while remaining pastors all along. Certainly, then it was no longer a question about "God's own word," and then all of a sudden it was a question of interpretation of Scripture. Isn't this what the opponents are going through now?

Now homosexuals (including pastors) want to have an official recognition of their partnership and have the church's blessing of their life together. They want to have legal rights and responsibilities towards each other. They want to promise love and respect to their partner, be faithful and loyal in thick and thin. For sure, this flies in the face of that *adversary image* one might have of homosexuals as promiscuous, loose, sensuality driven, and irresponsible individuals. Now when they seek recognition of their partnership they are no longer "outsiders" but part of the mainstream. The *adversary image* is fading out.

In the positive letters there is an added layer of care. The writers regard the expression of (homo)sexuality as a genuine expression of love equivalent to that of a heterosexual relationship. It is interesting that in the Swedish Church's debate over same sex-partnership the focus on love

---

1. Anders Frostenson hymn, Guds Kjærleik er som Stranda og som Graset (God's Love is like a Sea Shore and the Grass.

has been much more prominent than it has been in the debate in Norway. In the conversation document called "Homosexuality in the Church" published in 2003 by the Church of Sweden it states very clearly that conversations are futile unless they include the aspect of love. The document emphasizes how love is of great significance in every person's life. Love between partners—in spite of all misgivings—is a reminder of God's love. To be alive and to grow in close human contact is an essential part of being human. It is in relationship to others we learn about our own identity, it says in the document:

> Love is experienced just as significantly and formatively for homosexuals as it is for heterosexuals and by this we mean love in all its expressions. Should anyone in theory and in reality try to hinder or dissuade homosexual people from entering fulfilling love relationships that also take on a sexual expression, then it is equal to robbing homosexuals of a most significant element of human life. (page 13)

Two of the most often used arguments against same-sex-partnership in Norway is that the relationship is "contrary to the order of creation" and "contrary to God's word." The "order of Creation" refers to the creation story in Genesis 1, that reads "male and female he crated them" and it refers to words by Jesus in which two-gender relationships are taken for granted, thus implying that they are God-given (e.g. Matt. 19:3–9). Passages where homosexual behaviour is mentioned are as follows: Lev 18:22; and 20:13; Rom 1:24–27; 1 Cor 6:9–11; and Tim 1:9–11. In the Old Testament homosexual acts are punished by death (stoning). In New Testament references they are regarded as "disgusting," with the consequence that the people who commit such acts will not inherit the kingdom of God.

Undoubtedly the scripture passage cited most often, in the letters that is, is the one from Paul's writings in Romans 1:24–27.

> Therefore God gave them up in their lusts of their hearts to impurity, to the degrading of their bodies among themselves, because they exchanged the truth about God for a lie and worshipped and served the creature rather than the Creator, who is blessed forever! Amen. For this reason God gave them up to degrading passions. Their women exchanged natural intercourse for unnatural, and in the same way also the men, giving up natural intercourse with women, were consumed with passion for one another. Men committed shameless acts with men and received in their own persons the due penalty for their error.

The Image of God *and the Debate over Same-sex Partnership*

One letter writer refers to this passage as "God's crystal clear word."

Most of the people who quote this passage to show that same-sex relationship is a sin interestingly stop the quote at verse 27 (as above). However the rest of the chapter ought to be just as relevant, since this *catalogue of vices* as it is often called—continues with 'love of money', 'slander' etc. as examples of people living in opposition to God's word. To continue the list you find wickedness, envy, malice, strife, deceit, gossip and slander. Further you find people who hate God and use violence, are insolent, haughty, boastful, or are foolish, faithless, heartless, or ruthless (v29–31).

After this catalogue of vices no one can feel exempt from sin. What comes to my mind is the quote from Jesus: "the one who is without sin may be the first to throw a stone."

It is also interesting that those who quote this passage from Romans have no mention of the following chapter. Chapter 2 starts with a warning not to judge others. "For in passing judgement on another you condemn yourself, because you, the judge, are doing the very same things. You say 'We know that God's judgement on those who do such things is in accordance with truth'." (Rom 2:1–2) And the essence of Paul's letter to the Romans is precisely that we are justified by faith, not by works (acts).

THE CHURCH AND HOMOSEXUALITY

The question remains: With what authority it is possible to change policy when it comes to same–sex partnership. We are attempting to answer this question by drawing a parallel to two other controversial issues in the church over the last 50–60 years: divorce and re-marriage and the ordination of women.

Scripture is clearly against re-marriage, while there is a case for divorce according to Matthew and Paul. Never the less it has become a practise, also in the Church, against the writings of Scripture. About the ordination of women scripture is less specific, but it does speak about women's subordination in general as well as in matters of preaching, about keeping silent in the assembly. Today in the Norwegian church we have gone against this.

It was the same arguments that were brought up during the labour disputes at the start of the industrial revolution and again in the women's struggle for the right to vote. One of our bishops (J. C. Heuch) spoke in the national assembly in 1890 and said that women's voting right was against "God's clear word" and "the order of creation." He described how unbelief now was about to lead the entire nation into Hell, just like several of the negative letters held it.

Actually there are lots of similar 'turn-arounds' in church history. One of the most noticeable turns was the switch from Sabbath to Sunday as the "day of rest," which just happened at the very start of the church's history. In the Old Testament there was a death penalty (by stoning) for breaking of the Sabbath; (Numbers 15:32–36). The first Christians chose Sunday as a separate holy day because this day was the day of the resurrection. Actually then you have disregarded 'Scripture's strong command' for Jesus' sake. Scripture, The Old Testament at the time, is interpreted through the Jesus event. It is his life, example and words that decide which commands should be kept.

As just mentioned in this example it is necessary to have a key understanding of Scripture in order to use it for anything. Christian faith holds that Jesus' life and legacy is the interpretation key. This implies that not everything in The Bible is God's word—God speaking to the reader. In 1995 the College of Bishops in The Church of Norway stated the following:

> The final ethical conclusion must in the end be tested against "The Bible's genuine guide" (Luther), the crucified and risen Jesus Christ. There is always a danger that combinations of Biblical writings seemingly fit together but turn out graceless. We have historical evidence of such. The Church has used Bible passages as an argument against the abolition of slavery, against abolition of the death penalty, against social injustices, and against gender equality. Luther has taught us that the Bible contains God's word without being identical with God's word. A certain Scripture passage as well as any theological/ethical conclusion based on Scripture always gets its validity from coherence with Luther's Principle: "Was Christum treibt" (What leads towards Christ). The conclusion is that when the Church is to teach and guide in regards to homosexuality and same-sex partnership, then this must be congruent with its teaching about Jesus. (page 12)

So when anyone proposes a change in an established practice in the Church (and in society) and no longer follows "God's clear word" as an

The Image of God *and the Debate over Same-sex Partnership*

ethical principle, then it is based on the Jesus event (life and legacy) as a more accurate interpretation and ethical guide.

In 1997 a Church Convention decided that same-sex partnership is unacceptable for pastors and others who have a church ordination—catechists and deacons. Theologically speaking this is a very controversial decision, since it in fact operates with different standards (of sin) according to job status. In our opinion sin is sin regardless of status and job. There is no doubt that our Church is up a 'theological creek' in this decision, however it works as a pragmatic solution to a sensitive problem.

The decision is also on thin ice in its definition of "sin" when you consider same-sex partnership in the light of a fulfilling love relationship between individuals.

In the 1995 Bishop's Summit a minority group addressed the question of sin in regards to same-sex partnership:

> Since the Church advocates traditional marriage as a framework for expression of sexuality the homosexuals ask: Is same-sex partnership a sin? In order to answer such a question truthfully it is necessary to have a broad understanding of how 'sin' is used in the Bible. In the Bible 'sin' is not just about a person's behaviour or certain personal characteristics.
>
> Sin is first of all of a hyper-individual nature. Paul writes in Romans 3:23: "since all have sinned and fall short of the glory of God; they are now justified by his grace as a gift through the redemption that is in Jesus Christ." In John 16:9 Jesus said: "the sin is that they do not believe in me". This implies that there is no difference among people before God. Everyone is a sinner. Homosexuals are not greater sinners than others.
>
> Sin is also to go against God's will. To 'go against' implies a free choice.
>
> In matters of sexuality a person has a choice between two options that are not against God's will,—traditional marriage or singleness. The choice of marriage is not for everyone, but as long as it is an open option to live that way, there is a legitimate place for longings and dreams. The heterosexual singles will consequently feel their sexuality validated even though they choose not to live in sexual intimacy.
>
> This is different for persons with an absolute homosexual orientation. They are unable to choose heterosexual marriages. This sets up homosexuals for systemic confinement. Not even to have an alternative to sexual abstinence means that there is no room at all for dreams of and longings for sexual intimacy. As such they are

> deprived of feeling sexually validated. This further means that they are unable to feel validated as human beings.
>
> On this accord it is irrelevant to talk about 'sin' the way it is generally used. The question about whether same-sex partnership is sin cannot be answered. It is solely a matter between the individual's conscience and God. A same-sex relationship that is founded on loyalty and love has the moral quality that is genuinely Christian in nature.

I (R. K.) have to admit that I no longer feel good about the last paragraph in our statement from 1995; that the question about same-sex partnership as sin cannot be answered. I believe we positively must declare same-sex partnerships *not* to be sinful, provided they are based on genuine love just like we assume them to be when it comes to heterosexual partnerships. So we definitely take a leap of faith (for Jesus' sake) relative to what previously was regarded as "God's clear word." It is interesting to notice that these leaps often are about our view of humanity. And further it is amazing to ponder how many centuries it took to make Paul's words come true: "Here (in the Church, in the congregation) it is no longer Jew or Greek, slave or free, man or woman. For all of you are one in Christ Jesus" (Gal 3:28).

Looking at the positive letters in the debate it is interesting to notice how Scripture and reason work together in the deliberations over same-sex partnership. These people are in good company with Luther in this respect. Luther never advocated "Scripture alone" as a defence for his stand, his theology, but "scripture and reason" seeing that God has given us reason and logic to use for the good of all. Reason can help us read Scripture in the right way.

IDENTITY AND SEXUALITY

The way we look at homosexuality has changed. A brief review of just recent history will make this clear.

> Legislation about sexuality in general and homosexuality specifically has changed radically over the last 20–30 years. Up until 1970 homosexuality was disallowed and criminalized under section 213 of the Norwegian Criminal Code. Far into the 70-es homosexuality was looked upon as a disease. In USA it was taken off the list of psychiatric ailments in 1973, and in 1977 The Norwegian College of Psychologists proposed the same. In 1981 homosexuals were included as a group along with others to be exempt from

discrimination, and in 1993 we got a same-sex legislation allowing two persons of same gender to register their partnership as a permanent and committed union. Over a relatively short time period society's view and public opinion has made the situation different for homosexuals.[2]

At the same time there has been an increasing understanding of the relationship between sexuality and identity. As a psychologist I (S.S.) believe sexuality is a major and important part of our identity. The term 'gender identity' is in reference to a person's identity as a male or female and is most often a reflection on sexual orientation. Adult gays and lesbians have an identity as males or females.

> To identify with a certain sexual orientation is a rather new phenomenon in history and can be traced back to the nineteenth century. People act as if this distinction is a fixed boundary in the relationship between them, where as it in reality is a multivariable dynamic process[3].

Most sexologists of our time are of the opinion that every person has a heterosexual and a homosexual dimension to them. Both of these may be either strong or weak. In some cases only one is prominent while the other is in the background. These dimensions may vary independently of each other and of time and place. A sexual response to skin contact is general. As such most are potentially homosexual. However the degree of receptiveness to or rejection of one's own sensations varies from culture to culture. It may even be a cultural taboo in which case the culture can be identified as homophobic. What distinguishes homosexuality from heterosexuality is not homosexual behaviour, rather it is a lack of heterosexual interest. Regardless of upbringing and cultural influence a fully developed homosexual orientation will be deeply rooted in the personality and therefore not susceptible to alteration even if the person should wish to do so.[4]

Sexuality includes more than reproduction. Sexuality is about dreams, longings, and feelings. It is a comprehensive element of people's

---

2. Johnson, Norud, Magelsen, & Lappegard, Hvorfor mener vi det vi mener? Analyse av argumenter i homofilidebatten (Why do we believe what we believe? An analysis of the arguments in the debate over same-sex marriages). Hamar Diocese, 1997.

3. Arne Austad, *Seksuell identitet (Sexual Identity)*.

4. Preben Hertoft, *Klinisk Sexologi (Clinical Sexology)*.

life force and it has a great influence on how we experience our own being and worth. Homosexuals have the exact same needs as heterosexuals when it comes to intimacy and closeness.

Homosexuality has within the last 20–30 years gotten "a clean bill of health" after centuries of "chronic disease." Still homophobia is commonplace both in church and in society.

Homosexuality is still stigmatizing. The word *stigma* comes from Greek. Looking it up in a dictionary you will find this definition: "mark, brand, bodily wound; an identifying mark or characteristic—a specific diagnostic sign of a disease; bodily marks resembling the wounds of the crucified Christ sometimes accompanying religious ecstasy." It is ironic that stigmatizing is a reference to the way Jesus was treated with nails and a spear in his last moments. Perhaps it is possible to understand homophobia better by analyzing its origin. Many are of the opinion that education will eradicate all superstition and fear, and that more information about homosexuality will bring "light" to the oppression. However from experience we find that this doesn't always work. Perhaps we also need to re-examine our belief system and our ethics. Perhaps we need to look at our society and how it marginalizes people who are in a minority; the unbalance between rich and poor (North-South), family structure (the 'ideal nuclear family' hailed as Biblically inspired), our individual rights and responsibilities. This may be the way to achieve a greater tolerance, even respect. Respect must be part of our belief system, religious belief system and even our *image of God*.

THE CORE ISSUE

In Norway it was the controversy around the Siri Sunde case that started the public debate and sent people into a letter writing mode. What follows are the statements and documents from 1999, 'Faithful to the Truth in Love' to illustrate how I (R. K.) made my decision and to reflect what I believed the issue to be.

S. S. and R. K.

The Image of God *and the Debate over Same-sex Partnership*

CASE REVIEW—APPENDIX

(Original document from 1999)

'Faithful to the Truth in Love'

The so called 'Siri Sunde Case' has been a difficult issue that has touched many people in the Church of Norway and in our society in general. For this reason it is necessary to give a full explanation of both the content and of the process behind the decision made.

History

Siri Sunde was installed as a pastor in the parish of 'Nordre Land' on August 1996 after having filled a temporary call in the same parish since December 1995. In June 1997 she entered a same-sex partnership and on the same day she asked for a leave of absence following the advice of the Hamar bishop. She was granted the leave at first waiting for a Church Synod meeting about homosexuality in November of 1997, and next waiting for the bishop's appeal before the *Commission on Dogmatics*. October 8, 1998 the case was dismissed by the *Commission on Domatics* stating that this was an administrative matter leaving the bishop with the decision.

Out of respect for the statements from the Church Synod meeting, and for those who have an opinion different from mine, I was tempted to delay the matter even further. However it would be inconsiderate of me to let Siri Sunde be on a leave of absence for an unspecified length of time. The congregations of the parish affected by this also pressed for a speedy solution. I am fully aware that such a long leave of absence is a problem for the congregations.

What the Issue Is—And What the Issue Is Not

What the Siri Sunde case is about is whether a person in a same-sex partnership is allowed to be a pastor in the Church of Norway. The case is not about homosexuality in general. The general discussion has been the topic of a Bishop's meeting as well as a Synodical meeting and it has become apparent that in the church there are many diverging views concerning homosexuality. However everyone has agreed that the issue should not cause a split in the Norwegian Church.

Neither is the case about whether homosexuals are allowed to be pastors in the Church of Norway. Today there are a number of homosexuals working in the church, also in appointed offices, and the discussion about homosexuality has not altered this practice. Neither has anyone raised a theological issue that Siri Sunde being a lesbian is ineligible as a pastor. What it is all about is a pastor's right to enter a same-sex partnership.

Progress Towards a Solution

On my recommendation Siri Sunde asked for a leave of absence awaiting the decision of the Church Synod in the fall of 1997. The Synod declared homosexuals in partnership ineligible to hold 'called offices' in the Church. At the Synod there was a significant minority who did not share this opinion, but for the time being they agreed to follow the majority decision. Practically speaking, however, the Synod has neither a legislative nor a judicial power in church affairs. The Synod's document, which I take seriously, cannot overshadow the fact that it is I (the Bishop) who have the final responsibility to make a contextual evaluation and decision.

The road from there to a clarification of the matter is as follows:

—Sunde's leave of absence was extended after the Synod because I brought the matter before the *Commission on Dogmatics in the Church of Norway*. The rationale behind this was that I believed the Synod in a matter of doctrine had assumed an authority that rightly belonged to the *Commission on Dogmatics*. I asked that the Commission would "assess the dogmatic issue involved in the so called Siri Sunde case in Diocese of Hamar" and debate whether the Synod's distinction between 'called offices' and 'lay workers' was a true representation of Lutheran Theology. When the Commission dismissed the case on October 8, 1998 it was back in my court to make a decision.

—After the dismissal of the case I arranged a meeting with the chairpersons for the congregations in 'Nordre Land' parish to inform them of the situation and to invite their response in the process. We were in agreement that the congregations' attitudes were essential, and that nobody has a right to be a pastor anywhere if this leads to a split in the congregation. The leaders were asked to survey their congregational councils regarding Sunde's tenure as a pastor. It turned out that one council was negative, two were positive, and one stated that they would accept whichever decision was made. The support of the local congregations is necessary should she return to the job of being their pastor. Further there are two pastors in the parish, meaning that nobody is referred to Sunde exclusively.

—I consulted with the Church's Continuing Education and Research Department branch, The Church Secretariat for Employment and other lawyers. My wish was to sort through all legal and labour related consequences of the Synod's decision and of a possible firing of Sunde. The point here is that it is not about appointing a pastor to a parish but about firing a pastor. The legal ramifications surrounding a firing are outlined much better than in a case of hiring. The result of my consultation was not conclusive, but it is fair to say there was uncertainty and even a reasonable doubt about the Church's chance of winning a possible ensuing legal battle.

Had the case been about central Christian principles, it would be possible to make a case for the Church being exempt and different. In such a case it would automatically fall under a different category with special provisions for faith groups. However when the bishops are split, the Synod is divided in a majority and a minority, and the *Commission on Dogmatics* refused to speak on the matter, then it is difficult to claim that this case is so important for the church that the special not-withstanding clause should be used in regard to the general Norwegian laws e.g. labour laws. This is part and parcel of the final decision I had to make.

I also wanted to find out if there was a fiscal possibility of finding a so called "middle way," in this case for instance retraining to a special project or service in a specialized field. No extra funding was available, only reposting within the diocese's service area.

—In a meeting with "The Coalition for Gay & Lesbian Rights" and with "Church Open for All" I was especially interested in their reaction to different outcomes of this case. I voiced my concern over that if Siri Sunde kept her position this might create a backlash for homosexuals in several diocese, and over loosing everything that had been achieved through the Synod's pragmatic decision. They were very direct with me. Their experience was that the promised dialogue about homosexuals in the church had gone missing and that they didn't see the desired integration and equality policies materializing. To them Siri Sunde's case was of great symbolic consequences for all homosexual Christians. Foremost to them it was about being open and 'out of the closet' within the church.

—The pastors from the *Hadeland and Land* conference asked me to meet with them. I too was eager to talk to them about work relationships and about collegiality. For some time I have shared my dilemma in this case with most of the pastors in the diocese, as well as with the deans and the Council of the Diocese. In the *Hadeland and Land* conference the pastors were almost unanimous in their scepticism when it came to Sunde going back to her job. In the diocese in general there is a much wider spectrum of opinions and attitudes.

—After my consultation regarding labour laws I also wanted to meet with the politicians. I requested a meeting with the Minister of Church Affairs, *Lilletun*, and informed him about what had happened in the case so far. We examined the situation and debated possible solutions in a constructive manner.

—Of course there has been continuing contact and conversation with Siri Sunde and the local Labour Board. The conversations have touched on several solutions and options regarding rights and responsibilities of employees and employers. Reassignments within the church have been presented to Siri Sunde, but she maintains that she desires to be the parish pastor in *Nordre Land*.

A Broken Promise

A lot of people have approached me concerning Siri Sunde's broken promise to me about not entering a partnership as long as she was in office. I am sorry about the broken promise but I have not let that influence my decision in the case as it has unfurled. At the time we were both under severe stress but I later realized how inappropriate of me it was to request such a promise.

Theology and Partnership

I have once again examined the Biblical references and the theological reasoning concerning homosexuality; I included recent researchers' findings as well. I still hold it, as did the minority group at the Bishops Meting in 1995, that one cannot use any single scripture reference taken out of context as the basis for one's point of view in this matter. Each single reference must be interpreted according to an over all principle, just as it is done in other matters; for example in the matter concerning ordination of women.

Luther's guiding principal was 'What leads towards Christ' (Was Christum treibt). The applicability and validity of each scripture reference is up against the teaching, life, death and resurrection of Jesus—his

The Image of God *and the Debate over Same-sex Partnership*

entire mission. St Paul uses a phrase that captures this principle when he says "speaking the truth in love, we must grow up in every way to him who is the head, into Christ" Eph 4:15. My perception is that it all comes down to 'speaking the truth in love'. The way I read and understand Jesus' mission is a continuing solidarity with the outcast, the oppressed, and the ones who have suffered hardship. In word and in deed Jesus presents a surprising acceptance of his less fortunate fellow human beings: women, children, tax collectors, gentiles, Samaritans. This heartfelt accept and respect has to be the foundation for all theological reasoning.

In the same way the church has changed its position on other matters so now it must change its position on homosexuality. Using present day insight and knowledge we cannot in the name of love equate today's same-sex partnerships with the immorality to which St Paul is referring. Therefore there is no theological reason for excluding a person living in a same-sex partnership from working in the Church of Norway.

In my opinion the government's same-sex legislation is a morally responsible way of dealing with homosexuality in our society. The law provides homosexuals rights and responsibilities in civic matters appropriate to the common standards of a democratic society in terms of community, solidarity, mutuality, intimacy and love. I have not yet been convinced by any church organization that such a life is immoral. At a time when sexuality in some respects has not only been reduced to casual relationships but also been the object of commercialization it ought to be applauded by the church when homosexuals embrace committed partnership under civic legislation.

Throughout the debate in 1995 my conviction was that it is not right to exclude persons in a same-sex partnership from ordained ministry in the Norwegian Church. This point of view is shared by a not insignificant minority of pastors, bishops, and Synod delegates. This view is also in harmony with the majority's conclusion of the bishops' taskforce in 1995. In1997 the Synod introduced the distinction between lay and ordained persons working for the church as a pragmatic compromise, but this really is problematic in a Lutheran Church that advocates a 'priesthood of all believers' where baptism is the one fundamental act of ordination.

Relationship with The Synod

I have previously referred to the 1997 decision of the Synod that persons in a same-sex relationship cannot be on the clergy roster of the Church of Norway. In the process I first voted for my own motion—which was and still is that a person in a same-sex relationship may be on the clergy roster. When this motion was defeated I subsequently voted for the compromise which was designed to accommodate the opposing sides of the debate. At the time I was debating with myself whether I should vote for the compromise or not. In the end I decided to vote in favour in an attempt to maintain unity within the church. In retrospect it is important for me to note that church and congregation in essence do not depend on unanimity, but on the fellowship created by the proclamation of the Gospel of Jesus Christ and his love. Unity and unanimity in the Church are two completely different stories. It is a greater testimony to unity if partners can cooperate even if opinions are divided. The Synod's motion was never meant to be the final conclusion. It was intended to keep the conversation going. Consequently it was agreed to work diligently towards a different stance than what the Synod's compromise motion stated. However the compromise that we reached, and to which I so far was committed, has been sabotaged and undermined by the other group.

—A number of pastors have been backed up by their bishop in taking exemption to the compromise e.g. by refusing communion to same-sex partners.

—The desired conversation about integration with homosexuals has become silent.

—At the 1998 Synod the Synod itself circumvented its 1997 decision by rejecting a candidate (lay) in a same-sex relationship for a job for which he was very well qualified.

—It appears that having a positive view on same-sex partnership presently is being used as a disqualifying criterion in church advancement and nominations. This being the case means using the compromise about mutual respect to minimize the influence of the minority group.

My Stand

As the time has passed after the 1997 Synod compromise I have come to regret the way I voted. In short my dilemma was: I had supported the resolutions of the Bishops Meeting and of the Synod in regards to church employment of people in a same-sex partnership. I had done this out of fear that the church might split, and to give my contribution to the maintenance of church unity. Admittedly I have done this against my core belief as a person of faith and truth, a belief I have been contemplating for over 25 years. And as time has passed I have struggled with the question: What does it mean 'to be faithful to the truth in love'? Are there situations where truth is unbending to a majority decision? Are there situations where somebody must break established praxis and tradition in order to champion what you in your heart believe to be the truth based on what you have found from scripture and confessions? For me this is the case.

The Church has a lot to apologize for to the homosexuals. Far into the 20ith century the homosexuals were an ostracized and rejected group of people whom the church did not defend and care for as one might expect given the gospel's ethics and mission. In the light of a dark history it would be an important act of solidarity with the homosexuals and their struggle for the right to a respectable life if the Church's official voice supported the same-sex legislation of the government. This would include people in ordained ministry in the church.

I would like to point out the severe consequences of the status quo. There are several examples of persons in ordained ministry who have felt a pressure to leave their vocation because they met another person with whom they wanted to live in a same-sex relationship. We also have examples of pastors who feel pressured to hide their true sexual identity.

A great many people have been strongly engaged in this issue, and I have received a lot of communication about it. For many it has become a test of the church's authenticity, how it relates to people, whether people are included or excluded.

'RULES OF THE ROAD'

How is it possible for the church to manage a situation about which there will be different opinions for a long time? Majority and minority have to find a way in which they can accept the difference. Unity in the church does come about by a majority's veto against a minority's conscientious belief and its practical implications. Paying attention to the Church's unity is important to me. However it is hard to understand that church unity might depend on uniformity of praxis in a mater that in reality polarize the Norwegian church from top to bottom. The Church's unity centers on it's loyalty to the gospel that declares everyone a sinner and in need of God's grace. Everyone has the same worth as human beings, and has the same status in the church through baptism. In conclusion we must accept different praxis because we agree that it is not a church-splitting matter.

As an example of something similar it is obvious to recall the church's way of handling the issue of ordination of women. The Church of Norway has for years allowed women into ordained ministry, and the vast majority of the church has experienced this as an enhancement and victory for the gospel's authenticity. However in the church there is a conservative minority that does not recognize female clergy. This group has had the opportunity to keep its point of view in the church, has been and still is promoted to vital committees and taskforces and even appointed to become bishop overseeing women clergy. A certain protocol has been put in place to make it possible for the opponents of female clergy to follow their conscience in praxis.

In my opinion this grandiose gesture and tolerance exhibited by a liberal majority towards a conservative minority is a good example of what may facilitate unity in the church in a constructive manner. In order that the unity of the church should not be broken over the issue of same-sex partnership it is similarly necessary to establish guidelines and an etiquette to make room for both parties in the church. To develop these 'rules of the road' would be the jurisdiction of the bishops and the church employees' union.

ECUMENICAL CONSIDERATIONS

Our church's relationship to other churches has been used as an argument for exercising restraint when it comes to altering our view on clergy in a same-sex relationship. It is most obvious then to consider our sister churches in Sweden and Denmark, who have handled this issue much more openly than we have done so far. In both Sweden and Denmark there are pastors living in same-sex relationships, and the churches have found ways to accommodate this. Both culturally and historically these are the churches with whom we most adequately may compare ourselves.

The Image of God *and the Debate over Same-sex Partnership*

THE LEGAL IMPLICATIONS

To fully include homosexuals in the church it is essential that the church support the civic same-sex legislation and embrace it. I also want to be mindful of the level of security the church offers its employees.

I hold it that church employees should work under the same secure labour conditions as other employees. The labour laws are not to be considered an untimely interference in internal church affairs. If the church in the coming years wants to be taken seriously also as a reliable employer, it is paramount that it not only adheres to but also actively supports laws and regulations that already are in place to promote good working conditions for all.

The legal counsel I received points to the likelihood of Siri Sunde winning a legal battle over employment status should she be dismissed from her job. With all this in mind I find it impossible that I, with my deep held belief should be the one to trigger a legal battle that I do not support either theologically or judicially for an intended purpose of firing a pastor whom I am convinced is doing a good job.

CONCLUSION

I have now presented principal and practical grounds for my position in the case regarding pastors and same-sex partnership and Siri Sunde's tenure as the pastor of *'Nordre Land'* parish.

But the principle reason for my decision lies in Jesus' love and his inclusive conduct towards every human being.

I have therefore decided to let Siri Sunde return to her appointment as the parish pastor of *Nordre Land*. I appeal to the congregations, team-pastors and other workers in the church to receive her well.

Diocese of Hamar

R. K.
February 1, 1999

6

Destructive Religion

RELIGIOUS FAITH AND BELIEF can be liberating and life affirming but it can also do the exact opposite—be destructive. This was quite evident in the letters we reviewed in the previous chapter. Faith can provide life with energy and meaning, even be liberating; but it can also be rigid and exclusive.

The practice of a religion entails a pursuit of your innermost human longings and a desire to explore the numinous. This is in the very definition of the word *religion*. It comes from the Latin *religio, religiare* which means to tie the human quest for meaning to a divine power. In the words of theologian Dorothee Sölle:

> Religion is an attempt to interpret everything in the world away from alienation, hostilely, fatalism and meaninglessness. Rather it reframes everything so as to make it part of the human experience. Everything is "for us." Religion is an attempt to curb nihilism and decidedly to live life boldly.[1]

The positive aspects of religion can reduce existential anxiety. Religion can give hope, purpose and a sense of being safeguarded, protected. The positive side of a religious faith can entail solutions to ethical dilemmas, provide moral guidelines, enhance social interaction, satisfy the need for belonging and strength through ritual and communal participation, and give hope beyond death and misery. The negative side of religion can produce unhealthy guilt feelings, feelings of inferiority, produce unhealthy suppressions of anger, anxiety and fear of punishment e.g. fear of hell. It can disturb the sense of balance and purpose; create external dependence, conformity and corruption of the mind. The negative side of religion can hamper sexual expression, create division between the

---

1. Dorothee Sölle: *Choosing Life*.

saved and the unsaved, and a paranoia of evil forces. Destructive religion provides no framework for the process of growth and development in a lifelong search for authenticity. On the contrary it is deliberately used as a means of exercising authority over the adherents. The practice of this 'sort of religion' creates bondage and dependency, inferiority and denigration. Destructive religion produces anxiety and creates delusions. In short it can make an individual both physically and mentally sick.

Destructive religion is in this context used to describe (any) misuse of religion or a religious belief that causes damage to its adherents and 'faithful'. Actually it is an oxymoron to talk about destructive religion. Religion is per definition never destructive; only in its abuse is it destructive. Abuses are found in all religions, not only in Christianity. At times the abuse has been so massively poignant that people intuitively came to associate religion with something negative, life-limiting and mordacious—and not with something meaningful and life giving. Faith's life affirming quality was overshadowed by mal-practice and institutional abuse. As a result people often avoid everything that has to do with institutional religion and 'the baby is thrown out with the bathwater'. This is a common trend in contemporary western societies. One group of people become radical church critics perhaps even hostile towards the institution, others turn towards trendy spiritual practices (often of eastern origin), many distance themselves from anything that appears to be religious or perhaps keep a non-practising membership in the traditional church out of respect for an older generation. Most people get a vague, superficial and non-committal relationship to religion.

At times politics and religion form an alliance to promote the status quo which often means legitimizing the already existing political systems and structures of society. Destructive religion can be used as a means governance and control.

MARTIN LUTHER AS A PATIENT

Historically speaking there is a rather well-known example of 'Christianity's shadow side'. The reformer Martin Luther experienced 'destructive religion' on a very personal level.

In his writings Luther has described how he feared the notion of 'falling into the arms of the living God'. This led him to an intense search of scripture and an equally intense search of his soul before he eventually arrived at a new paradigm: God is gracious! Luther was so to speak internally reformed before he set out to reform the institutional church. This is a story of healing. Luther overcame the destructive beliefs and the distorted *image of God* he had learned in his childhood at home and at school. Kierkegaard, the Danish theologian, says: 'Luther is for Christianity an extremely important patient'. Luther had a cognitive knowledge of the concepts of justification and re-conciliation. However, this did not mean he had overcome the feelings of eternal condemnation and guilt associated with sinning.

> In the Papal Church I fled from Christ and trembled at the mention of his name. In my heart I had the impression that he was a judge, to whom I would be summoned on the last day for an account of everything I'd said and done; but I knew those passages (that talked about God's mercy through Christ) and I read them daily without comprehension, for to me Christ was the judge.[2]

Martin Luther experienced the Papal Church as an exterior parallel to the inner 'papacy' that dictated his psychological functioning. His internalized *image of God* mainly came from the relationship he had with his father who was described as being very strict and authoritarian. The experience formed his personality which again determined how he read the Biblical passages.

> Once again the religious problem arises out of a psychological tension between the concepts, experiences and circumstances that guided the formation of Luther's personality and the insight (revelation) that met this inner world. Luther's theological training and studies hardly had any affect on his self-identity until he managed to externalize his painful inner world; that is: His introspection made him aware of the difference between a God revealed in Jesus of Nazareth and the God he had been given through his upbringing.[3]

This is an important psycho-religious mechanism that led to a monumental change in Luther's identity and self-awareness. From a fearful shivering at the mention of God's name he now felt like he had been 'born again'. His concept of God shifted dramatically since Scripture now revealed a new *image of God*.

---

2. Erik Erikson: *Young Man Luther.*
3. Ralf Ditlef Kolnes: *Åbenbaring og opplevelse (Revelation and Experience)* 214.

Destructive Religion

Destructive religion or belief oppresses and humiliates individuals by over emphasizing that they are sinful and weak. People who have been exposed to a destructive influence of this kind find it difficult to take care of their own interests and needs, to stand up for their own rights, and to follow their own dreams and ideas. Often they are stuck in unhealthy childish behaviours. They remain infantile and fail to take responsibility for their own life. Such an attitude to life is an impediment to independent and authoritative actions, and may often produce a depressive state of mind; the person feels a chronic guilt and provides a constant excuse for even being alive. Self-sacrificing, over-accommodating and ego-deprived people are easier to manipulate than people who are confident and self aware. In extreme cases, religion may push people into self-flagellation or even suicide for the religious cause. A religious neurosis may develop. At that point the religion becomes a fuel for a person's destructive behaviour against him/herself.

RELIGIOUS NEUROSIS

It is evident that a religious belief or practice can produce feelings of guilt, anxiety, and inferiority and a waning appetite for life. Such cases constitute a neurosis—a mental state that interferes with life in a negative way albeit not causing alterations in the nervous system. Since the 1950s clinical psychology and psychiatry have used the term 'ecclesiastical neurosis' (*ecclesia* is a Greek word for church, thus meaning 'church related neurosis'. In today's terminology we prefer the term 'religious neurosis' since these psychological phenomenon not only are found in the Christian community but in any religious system. The term thus summarizes all forms of religious, spiritual and psychoneurotic illnesses caused by damaging types of religion and spirituality. It makes sense to understand the religious neurosis as a private (personal) form of religion, more specifically as a regression to an early and situational specific developed religion.

The person who doesn't gain age-adequate insights, maturity, and personal integration inevitably develops some kind of neurosis. Typically this goes back to early childhood experiences but everything that happens throughout life has an effect—for better or worse. We cannot "just live life" without reflecting on it, working through losses and rising above eating, drinking, sleep and work. Suppose a person does not strive towards being the best he/she can be; then everyone looses—including the person him/herself.

Our spiritual development is an extremely important element in the development of our personality. In a lecture addressed to a group of clergy in 1932 C.G.Jung related his observations based on many years of practising psychotherapy:

> Among all my patients in their second half of life—that is after 35 years of age—none avoids having an issue with their religious/spiritual experiences. Actually they all become ill as a result of their religion's failure to sustain them—as religion is supposed to do. And none gets well again until they have found a new spiritual understanding—which may be quite different from creed or dogma or belonging to a certain faith/church group.[4]

There are certain types of religious neuroses:

a) *The Right Faith.*

b) *Moralism*

c) *Escapism*

d) *Reactive Atheism.*

These types of religiosity are often intertwined in the neurotic personality and it is not always easy to identify what is healthy and what is neurotic. Characteristically the level of energy required to uphold the religious platform is a good indicator. The more flexible and relaxed—reflective/spiritual—the more authentic and healthy. It seems to support the person's life. The more rigid, and authoritarian—legalistic/fundamentalistic—the more neurotic. It seems to consume the person's life force.

a. The Right Faith. Göran Bergstrand a Swedish writer, minister and therapist has described the 'unshakable faith'. According to him this is a defence and protection against anxiety and inner difficult conflicts. The religious neurosis covers up a more profound conflict. To keep this 'bubbling and simmering volcano' from erupting "the unshakable faith" is created—to use an expression used in spiritual direction. Its main attribute is its certainty and rejection of doubt. Doubt is regarded as dangerous and as a lack of character, even as stupidity. The 'rock-solid faith' is often supported by a complex structure of theology that has a straight logic character. Submission to certain fundamental ideas and authoritative

---

4. C. G. Jung, *Die Beziehungen der Psychotherapie zur Seelsorge.*

principles—clearly set apart from other 'minor ideas and principles'—is extremely important. As a consequence of this headstrong approach you often detect an emotional coldness towards others and a lack of ability to empathize and identify with others. An aggressive attitude is evident. There is a desire to debate and convince. They give long Biblical quotations and explanations of these instead of having a conversation and dialogue about living a life of faith. What is most important to them is to convert the other. The World is to be converted, but ironically they have great difficulty in reaching others because the aggressive undertones seem frightening and repulsive to most people.

Jonas Gardell, who is a self-declared homosexual, gives in his book *About God* the following anecdote. He describes an experience where he wanted to take communion (in the Lutheran Church of Norway).

> Well, it has happened. Strangers have literally put themselves between God and me with their bodies, as if they had to protect God against someone as disgusting as myself, and they have stared me straight into the eyes and screamed: "God hates and condemns you! God hates and condemns you!"—the Body of Christ is not given for me, his blood is not shed for me, I am locked out of his love— "God hates and condemns you." But that is not so! It is not consistent with what my mother in Enebyberg told me about God.[5]

Representatives of 'The Right Faith' often have a strong opinion about how to read the Bible and about what actions are characteristic of a life of faith.

> As a reflection of their specific religious up-bringing all Christians are faced with a choice in the way they relate to God. It may seem as if the fundamentalists, those who uncritically believe every word of the Bible and who do not notice any contradictions in it, have the most heartfelt faith and the greatest resource of religious role-expectations all based on their detailed knowledge (often memorized) of the Bible.[6]

A spokesperson for 'The Right Faith' almost always considers him/herself to be a co-worker with God. Everything has a purpose, and God has singled him/her out for a special purpose. This may produce people who

---

5. Jonas Gardell: *Om Gud* (*About God*), 9.
6. Eystein Kallestad: *Gjennom det menneskelige til det guddommelige* (*Being Human Becoming Divine*), 22.

are very action-oriented but also people who are intolerant towards those of a different opinion. 'The Right Faith' rests on some form of fundamentalism. Gunnar Stålsett has written a fine description of the aspects associated with fundamentalism:

> Firstly fundamentalism is *intolerant*. It is based on the assumption that this faith and religion is the only truth. Secondly it is *political* in that it justifies violence as an expression of faith. Thirdly, it is *counter-contemporary* and resists everything 'modern and secular'. Fourthly it is *authoritarian* and demands total allegiance to its doctrine and scriptural interpretations. Fifth it seems like *male dominance* is an element in all fundamentalism. Last but not least it is *anti democratic*. It denies basic democratic values such as equality of race, gender, and religion, and it rejects freedom of choice for both individuals and groups.[7]

In reality the people of 'The Right Faith' are deeply insecure. To compensate for this their 'faith" becomes a psychological crutch. It supports and gives strength where otherwise it would collapse and fall to the ground.

b. Moralism. The religious neurosis is frequently characterized by a preoccupation with morals. This is not to say that these persons have high moral standards. What it does mean is that the religious neurotic consistently suppresses anxiety, vulnerability, sexuality, and aggressive tendencies and as such creates an image of uprightness. They easily 'see the speck in their neighbour's eye but fail to see the log in their own'; they are unaware of their own non-acceptable tendencies and impulses. To an outsider they show a facade that is quite the opposite of what they cannot accept in themselves. The one who holds back his aggressions becomes overly friendly, the vulnerable shows incredible strength, and the one who cannot accept his own sexuality becomes prim and proper. Occasionally the very chaos you are trying to curb will appear in yourself in the form of impulses of an aggressive or sexual nature. Some very pious Christians are of the opinion that in order to stay pure and continually live a charitable life you must suppress your natural impulses, especially sexual and aggressive inclinations.

To keep these forbidden areas of life away from you the person defends him/herself by using isolation and suppression. Intellectually this may even be supported with religious doctrine. However the things suppressed from the conscious mind seeks to be expressed in some way.

---

7. Gunnar Stålsett: *Hva er da et menneske? (Who's a Human Being then?)*, 116.

Destructive Religion

The pious may have obsessions about 'the forbidden' content and perhaps even fall into despair over these 'tainted fantasies'. Neurotic religious moralism often takes the form of seeing sinful tendencies and nasty intentions in other people, and then pointing it out with disgust. When they get a chance to accuse others of moral failure their own sense of guilt diminishes. This seems to be a reasonable explanation for their condescending and judgemental attitude towards others. It supports a frail self-esteem.

But what is denied cannot be kept away forever. It surfaces as anxiety, prejudice and projection. *Projection* is a subconscious psychological mechanism. The unknown and subconscious part of our personality is transferred to other people so we in them see what in reality is part of our own personality. This may have a very negative influence on personal relationships. When we meet people and have negative feelings towards them, it is important to stop up and ask ourselves if this negative feeling perhaps is due to something we don't like in ourselves; meaning that we just projected it onto the other person. This is not always the case, but sometimes it is. And when it is the case our relationship with the other person is seriously damaged by our own subconscious self. This is one way in which prejudice comes into existence.

How then in a certain situation is it possible to detect and realize that projection is at play? First and foremost we get in touch with our subconscious self (shadow side as Jung calls it) when we have unwarranted and exaggerated feelings towards another person (envy, hatred, aggression). At that point we are actually looking straight at our own suppressed or inferior feelings reflected in the other person. An example. As mentioned before people who hold back their aggressions may become over accommodating or obliging in order to hide their 'true selves'. Now, if you meet another person who is very accommodating or charming this may trigger strong emotions with you because you have adopted this very defence mechanism against your own aggressive self. So you overreact to charm because in your life charm means 'hidden aggression'.

Even when we realize that projection is taking place it is still hard to deal with it on a profound level. However it is necessary to do so to become a mature integrated person. Ruth Poort a Danish psychiatrist puts it this way:

> Nobody is a better preacher of penance than the one who has to seek absolution for his/her own nature and who in this way can re-

deem him/herself by taking offence at other people's sinful nature. The crows hang out where there is a carcass.

Nobody is more critical than the one who is weak and therefore needs to put others down to elevate him/herself.

Nobody becomes an obsessive-compulsive neurotic person except the one who has strong passions and personality rifts so that ritual and obsessions may guard against them.

Nobody can get as jealous of two people who love each other and make each other happy as can the one who longs for someone to love and care about.

Nobody can take offence at another person as can the one who has not lived a good life and now realizes it is too late.

Nobody's human condition is more tragic than the one who discovered he/she forgot to accompany his/her shadow and therefore didn't live a full life.[8]

c. Escapism. Escape from reality is another aspect of the religious neurosis. The 'escape' often goes back to a very early stage in life when you lived in carefree dependence with responsible adults. It is virtually a regression; you revert to attitudes that you should have outgrown long ago. The demands of the adult world appear to be too demanding to deal with. One common aspect of the neuroses is that they are attempts to avoid a real encounter between the world and the person. From the perspective of a person reverting to an earlier stage it is important that religion keeps its sheen of 'happiness' and nobody alters the 'childhood faith'. This kind of 'faith frozen in time' is not a life giving faith, rather it gives the person a desire to shut out the real world and to nestle into a 'comfortable churchy incubator' where an intravenous word of God is fed right into the bloodstream. You don't live life to the fullest; just surviving; hoping that life on the other side of death eventually will be better than this.

Individuals suffering from a neurotic escape from reality often have a longing for Paradise; a longing that is not primarily theologically founded. Rather it is a longing for nourishment and comfort from someone who never lets you down. Consequently they never take responsibility for their own life, they never become emotionally mature, and remain in an unhealthy dependency of others. In Norway many Free-Churches attract these people as these churches are of a more fundamentalist and hierarchal nature. They do not ask questions. They have a Bible base and ask no questions about the Bible either. The Bible is a God-given book. It

---

8. Ruth Poort: *Psykologien som tjener (Psychology to Serve You)*.

is God's direct word with no human interference. They dismiss the idea of any possible human influence on its wording or presentation. In addition these communities have strong charismatic leaderships—father figures who take care of everything. The God-concept becomes intertwined with the person's relationship to the church's official representative, and in this mixture God becomes an authority, judge, and perhaps unscrupulous avenger. You have to abide by the rules of the community or else leave the community. Us or them. An exclusive group.

In chapter five we looked at the letters received by the bishop's office. Some mentioned God's punishment to the extreme. Some of the writers may have been exposed to Biblical 'brainwash' in early childhood or later in Sunday school. They have been overwhelmed with images of Judgement Day at a time when they were very receptive, and probably by people whom they trusted. This would most certainly result in issues of trust and insecurity later in life. The most troublesome issue is likely the lingering feelings of profound guilt and fear. Not only are they under their parent's scrutiny but they are likely to also get God's punishment and that just for being ordinary children wanting to have fun, play games, joke around, dance and explore the world. Certain families label this as sinful and frown upon anything that is 'fun'. The result of this form of upbringing varies greatly, but in some cases it may lead to psychological disturbances; for instance if this happens early on and to a high degree then the person may need extended therapy to overcome the negative impact this may have had. Quite often the negative *images of God* have been presented with great pathos and graphic imagery and found a fertile ground giving growth to further fantasies and anxieties. Later in adult life this may produce huge amounts of anxiety about death, something we have often encountered in hospital conversations. Fear of death and fear of life are connected.

This kind of early impact with an authoritarian *image of God* has almost made it impossible for the person to develop any other way. They are locked into this negative judging *image of God*. Later in adult life when they meet people and especially church officials, who use Bible verses that are different from what they know or interpret the texts in a different way or even talk about God in ways that are unfamiliar to them, well, then it upsets them greatly and they feel their 'childhood faith' is under attack. This gives insecurity; like the rug is pulled away under them; they become angry. They have grown so accustomed to reading the 'signs of the coming judgement' that they only see this as another sign. Everything but what they are familiar with is labelled as 'Anti-Christ' and the cycle repeats itself once again.

d. *Reactive Atheism* may be another aspect of a religious neurosis. For a person who grew up in a family where God was the ultimate answer to everything, and where the child was supposed to keep quiet while exposed to more or less incomprehensible undertakings (long worship services and sermons) it is quite common that the *image of God* becomes the one of a "Big Brother." A Sunday school song comes to my mind: "Oh, be careful little eyes what you see, For the Father up above Is looking down in love," For a child 'looking' is the main message, even though the song says 'looking in love'. God is constantly watching, always awake, and sees everything. For some individuals this *image of God* may lead to a religious neurotic anxiety.

There are several ways in which a person may react to this form of anxiety. You may rebel against your parents and their authority, God, and by so doing shake off God as well as the parents. This may create strong ambivalent feelings. On the one hand you need to get rid of your dislike for the ever scrutinizing and spying God; on the other hand you want to keep the feelings of security and comfort the parents had found through their faith. This is called a 'reactive atheism' or an 'inverse faith'. To avoid the attraction of an authoritarian God you become a militant atheist. The low self esteem is compensated through a high need for revenge. "The headstrong mindset is obvious and may develop into a mental armour that supports the entire personality"[9]

To summarize this chapter's many different aspects of a religious neurosis it may be said that this is all part of what we earlier called *godpoisoning*. When religious faith becomes destructive and harmful to an individual—when it hampers the wellbeing, creates irrational anxiety and feelings of guilt—then it works like a poison.

When it is called *godpoisoning* and identified as such it makes it easier for the person to become liberated from the neurosis. The neurosis, the mental illness, is diagnosed, has a specific cause and is not self inflicted due to poor choices and ignorance; rather it is caused by others and the environment in which the person was raised. At any rate from our experi-

---

[9]. Owe Wikström: *Stöd eller börda? (Support or Burden?)*.

ence the naming process has been helpful to many and helped them to get on with their life in a new way.

In the chapter on spiritual development we tried to describe the complex relationships between personality development and the many issues that have to be dealt with at each stage of development. We have also analyzed how profoundly the negative (or positive) *image of God* is imprinted on the person's psyche, and exactly for that reason is so difficult to alter later in life. A negative *image of God* produces anxiety and so does change. The person prefers the known anxiety over an unknown anxiety even if this may lead to no anxiety at all.

As a help towards detoxification and as an aid in changing a negative *image of God* the last chapter of this book rolls out fifteen positive and life affirming images of God taken from the Christian tradition. As this is our own background we feel comfortable doing this. Perhaps someone from another faith tradition could supplement this. We believe that a positive *image of God* is found in all major religious traditions of the world. The next chapter however is an exploration of the Gospel according to Matthew as an example of how the author historically and contextually portrayed Jesus of Nazareth as an *image of God*.

In his answer to the question "what is God?" German theologian Dietrich Bonhoeffer says:

> Not a general faith plain and simple, but a meeting with Jesus Christ. because Jesus totally exists for others. To come in touch with this about Jesus "to-be-living-for-others" is to experience the transcendent.[10]

S. S.

---

10. Dietrich Bonhoeffer: *Wiederstand und Ergebung*, 220.

7

"The Exact Imprint of God's Very Being" —Matthew's Jesus

An Incarnation Study

IN CHAPTER TWO WE stressed that all talk about God is couched in imagery. Some writers like Helge Svare advocate that the life of Jesus in the way the New Testament is written is a metaphor for God or for the Kingdom of God. My own question is: Aren't we beyond the metaphor when it comes to Jesus? The book of Hebrews in the New Testament opens with the statement that Jesus is the *imprint* of God's very being (v 3). Meanwhile John's Gospel goes a bit further and says: "no one has ever seen God. It is God the only Son who is close to the Father's heart, who has made him known." (John 1:18)—Or more directly translated: "who has made exegesis—interpretation—of him." In other words: Is our talk about God also metaphorical when we use theological language and talk about the incarnation as it was done at the council of Nicaea back in 325: "true God and true man" or in the words of the Creed "true God from true God, begotten, not made, of one Being with the Father" Haven't we gone further then? "And the Word became flesh and lived among us" (John 1:14). In Jesus' life we have a demonstration of how God is and acts physically and concretely. In some way we leap from image and conceptual idea to real presence, God's presence.

A more dubious consequence of the incarnation theology is this: Since God did not come to us as a daughter but as a son, then this means that God is male (see chapter two). When Jesus is not the son of Joseph then it is because The Father is his father. Logically God is not the mother since Jesus already has a mother, Maria. This means then that to talk about,

"The Exact Imprint of God's Very Being"—Matthew's Jesus

even to address, God as a woman is ludicrous. God is male; nothing more than comparable to a mother. In conclusion: God is male. All twelve disciples were male. All clergy must be male. To me this kind of logic short circuits the outcome. Irregardless of this I still want to be your guide on a journey through the Gospel according to Matthew for the purpose of illustrating Matthew's *image of God* as he sees it in the life of Jesus.

In the Bible there are four life-stories about Jesus, the Gospel according to Matthew, Mark, Luke and John each with its own characteristic. How exciting that is. Here I have picked Matthew's version for a study. It is written around year 80 C.E. and addressed to Christian congregations in Northern Palestine in the area bordering Israel and Syria. What has Matthew chosen to emphasize, what is his picture of Jesus—and ultimately of God? I have chosen nine vignettes—puzzle pieces—to form the larger picture. Kind of enigmas in the story that subtly hints at Matthew's understanding of Jesus.

FIRST VIGNETTE: THE WOMEN OF THE FAMILY TREE (MATTHEW 1)

For most people the most boring parts of the Bible are the endless lists of ancestry. Often we do not even bother reading them. In the case of Matthew's Jesus-story however, it represents a significant amount of theological insight. In a long list of male ancestors (patriarchal society) Matthew inserts four women other than Jesus' mother Maria: Tamar, Rahab, Ruth, and Uriah's wife (Bathsheba). This is most unusual. In Luke's story there are only male names in Jesus ancestry. In the Old Testament and in Jewish tradition in general only the male ancestors are mentioned.

Furthermore, it is interesting which four women are the ones included in the story. Tamar's story is told in Genesis chapter 38; she is a childless widow (twice) who 'tricks' her father-in-law to conceive her child. In some Jewish writings she is looked upon as non-Jewish; but to Matthew it is her great merit that she secures the lineage from the patriarch Abraham to King David. About Rahab the Book of Joshua (chapter 2 and 6) tells that she was a prostitute who helped the Israelites conquer the city of Jericho by hiding the spies. According to Jewish tradition she is not included in David's ancestry, rather regarded as an example of a gentile (non-Jew) who comes to believe (see Heb 11:31 and Jas 2:25). In other words another woman of dubious origin and sexual morality.

Ruth is a Moabite, non-Jewish (Book of Ruth). In a cunning way she gets married to Boaz and their child Obed is David's grandfather. So she is the matriarch of the David dynasty and in rabbinic tradition she is the arch-mother of Messiah born of the House of David. The mention of Uriah's wife (Bathsheba) in the genealogy is a bit of a mystery too. You wonder why Matthew makes a point of doing this. Is it to emphasize her non-Jewish origin—wife of the Hittite Uriah—or is it her unfaithfulness to the husband? The story goes that she and David had a sexual encounter even though she and Uriah were married (2 Sam 11).

In short it is a quite peculiar gallery of women Matthew brings out for the readers of the genealogy. What they all have in common is the exemption from normal sexual behaviour of the time and that none of them were 'pure Jews'. Non-Jewish people/gentiles and people of mixed marriages were considered 'unclean' and association with them was forbidden for the orthodox Jew. Professor N.A. Dahl (Faculty of Theology, University of Oslo) writes in his Matthew-commentary: "Matthew had to mention a woman—Maria, the mother of Jesus. She was according to rumour and reputation not a good card. By selecting these other women in the ancestry, Matthew poses a counter argument to Maria's reputation by showing that God also in the past had inserted irregularities in the royal line—the line that 'in the fullness of time' would bring forth the Messiah. God brings about his will in spite of breaches to the norms and regulations he has given to his people. It is the despised, the unclean women who deliver the rescuers of the family line. They demonstrate how God's choice is sovereign and how God's plan for Israel throughout history and now through Maria is purely an act of love for humanity."

So, in other words, Matthew's first chapter—the genealogy—is a preview. It hints at who God's Kingdom is intended for and at what God's own nature is like. It represents an *image of God* that many orthodox believers would find offensive, while at the same time being a liberating force to others, people who were struggling with faith and life. In the end it leads to Jesus on the cross; first and foremost it was and is about the *image of God* that came with Jesus.

"The Exact Imprint of God's Very Being"—Matthew's Jesus

SECOND VIGNETTE: FROM POWER TO POWERLESSNESS. (MATTHEW 4:1-11)

And so we move on to the next stop on the journey. The story of Jesus' Temptation. The story goes that Jesus was tempted by the devil three times, and the third time it ends with:

> Again the devil took him to a very high mountain and showed him all the kingdoms of the world and their splendour; and he said to him, "All these I will give to you, if you will fall down and worship me." Jesus said to him, "Away with you, Satan! for it is written, 'Worship the Lord your God, and serve only him.'"

The phrase "Away with you, Satan" appears almost word for word again in another context later in Matthew's story, at the point where Jesus makes the first prediction of his suffering and death. (Matt 16:21 . .). The exasperated Peter says: "God forbid it, Lord! This must never happen to you." Jesus answered: "Get behind me, Satan!" When you read through Matthew's story it is obvious that Jesus' path is not one of power, but of suffering and the cross. (See also 17:22 and 20:17–19). This was absurd and contrary to Messianic expectations of the time, and even so offensive and humiliating that it took several hundred years before Jesus was depicted on the cross by any artist. The earliest known picture of Jesus on the cross is from around 430 and is found on the church door of St. Sabina in Rome.

Messiah, the King who is Coming, must be (all)mighty. He would 'rule over Israel'. He would 'crush the cruel rulers', 'cleanse Jerusalem from idol worship' and 'in righteousness abolish the sinners from their inheritance, and crush the haughtiness of the sinners like vessels of clay'. Quotes are from Solomon's Psalm 17 (apocrypha) which was written around 63 B.C.A. at the time the Romans invaded Palestine. Messianic expectations and the Jesus story were on a collision course.

The death of Jesus is an event in history; it is mentioned in sources other than the New Testament. The reason why he was executed in a (at the time) most cruel fashion is another question.

Was he brought to death as a political activist, a rebel? At the time there were a number of rebel movements in Palestine, e.g. the Zealots who continually antagonized the Roman occupation forces. The sign on Jesus' cross points to this. It said: INRI, a Latin abbreviation for Jesus of Nazareth, King of the Jews.

Or was it perhaps that he meddled with the religious authorities and became intolerable for the orthodox Jews who then handed him over to the Romans? Or that he pointed out how the Torah (rules of conduct) did not suffice in fulfilling God's will? Jesus also latched on to the prophetic critique of the sacrificial system. Like the prophets of old he declared that God wants compassion and justice among people, not sacrifices.

One can't help but notice how the writers of New Testament were struggling with the puzzle of Jesus' death, and how much attention all of the gospel writers give to the last week of Jesus' life. It is obvious that they try to understand. Along with the why-question there is another question of the same sort: Who is responsible for Jesus' death? Is it the Jews who handed him over to Pilate? Is it the Romans who actually executed him? Astoundingly they all arrive at the answer: No, everyone is responsible. Gerd Theissen[1] in his book about the social context of the early Christian church put it this way: "The execution of Jesus was a measure used by the Romans in their repressive policies. However it did not trigger hostility against the Romans from the Jesus followers. They accepted the defeat. The cross became a symbol of salvation, a sign—not of Roman cruelty—rather of humanity's shortcomings: Jesus had to die for our sake."

Matthew like the others is looking for a way to interpret the events. He finds it in scripture—Isaiah and his description of 'the man of sorrow'. He quotes Isaiah chapter 42 and 53 (see Matt 8:16–17 and 12:17–21). Isaiah chapter 53 is about vicariousness, vicarious sacrifice, that a person steps into a situation on behalf of another and assumes the suffering, guilt, and punishment that the other should have assumed himself:

> He was despised and rejected by others;
> a man of suffering and acquainted with infirmity;
> and as one from whom others hide their faces
> he was despised, and we held him of no account.
> Surely he has borne our infirmities and carried our diseases;
> yet we accounted him stricken, struck down by God, and afflicted.
> But he was wounded for our transgressions, crushed for our iniquities;
> upon him was the punishment that made us whole,
> and by his bruises we are healed. (Is 53:3–5)

A closer look at this figure in Isaiah reveals a juxtaposition of deliverance from injustice and captivity with deliverance from sin and guilt.

---

1. Gerd Theissen, *Jesus. Overleveringen og dens sociale baggrund (Jesus. The Oral Tradition and The Social Context)*.

"The Exact Imprint of God's Very Being"—Matthew's Jesus

The same dual purpose is attributed to Jesus in all the gospel stories. He frees people from sickness and death. He promises justice to the poor. And he absolves people of their sins. He takes away their guilt. What is termed salvation is a comprehensive human experience. It is for body and soul. It annuls the power of death.

Jesus' death is a fact. The narrative is an interpretation. In the language of theology it is about a God who loves the human beings he created, who loves his enemies; about a God who does not 'brake a bruised reed or quenches the smouldering wick' (Matt 12:18–19). It is about a God who gave himself for humanity.

THIRD VIGNETTE: THE GALILEE OF THE GENTILES (MATTHEW 4:12–16)

Matthew is the only gospel writer who mentions that Jesus moved to "the Galilee of the Gentiles" when he moved from his hometown of Nazareth to the border town of Capernaum by the Sea of Galilee. This is important for him, and he uses a quote from the prophet Isaiah to make the point. Galilee was an area with a 'mixed' population. It was conquered by the Assyrians in 733 B.C.A. and did not come back to Jewish control until 163 B.C.A. At that time apparently only a small part of its population was Jewish. When Jesus was alive, Galilee was under the rule of Herod Antipas 4 B.C.A.–39 C.A. (son of Herod the Great). It experienced a renaissance under him and even further after the fall of Jerusalem in 70 C.A. During the following centuries this was the birthplace of important Jewish literature. Foreign influence in this area is also attributed to the presence of the well known caravan route between Mesopotamia (today's Iraq) and Egypt. Just outside Capernaum there was a Roman garrison and customs office. At the time of Jesus Jews from Galilee were treated with scepticism by those of Jerusalem, because they were less observant of the traditional Jewish way of life. In other words it was not 'kosher' for an orthodox Jew to live in The Galilee of the Gentiles at Jesus' time.

It is appropriate to look at the word 'gentile'. In Jewish terminology a gentile (*goy*) is anyone who is born of a non-Jewish mother, impure because he is outside the Mosaic Law. Gentiles (*goyim* in plural) is a general reference to a group of people (a nation) just like '*am* when it is used for the nation Israel. A number of rather strict rules governed the day to day relationship with non-Jews and especially their access to the Temple. A Jew was to avoid contact with anything unclean; of gentile origin. Association with Gentiles was not allowed, e.g. you were not allowed to pay a visit to their home or eat with them, not to engage in commerce or to receive gifts from them, and certainly not to get married to them. According to one of the rules: "Anyone who professes to be of the Pharisee Brotherhood does not sell either fish nor dried fruit to a Gentile, buys no drink from him, does not stay as a guest in his house nor receive him as a guest in one's own house." Another rule says: "If anyone buys a household item from a Gentile he must wash it the usual way for purification, cook with it the usual way and temper it the usual way"[2]

The background for these rules is a certain theology, which is based on the belief that the Jewish nation is in a unique relationship with God. It is God's chosen people, and it is to be a holy people, a people who keeps the Law of Moses. Israel's identity was governed by the Law and to maintain this identity you would stay away from anything unclean. When factions of the Jewish society at Jesus' time tried to enforce the Law all the more, the clear intention was to create the 'True Israel' and thus bring in the 'Kingdom of God'.

It is interesting how the construction of the Temple at Jesus' time illustrates this. It was a magnificent complex in white marble, surrounded by an outer and an inner courtyard. The outer courtyard, which was for the Gentiles, had a solid wall around it with a beautiful cowered arcade. This was the place you could buy animals for sacrifices and exchange money to the special temple currency. This courtyard was open to everyone and at the religious festivals it was crowded with thousands of people. The inner courtyard was separated from the outer courtyard first by a six foot wall and then by another nine foot wall. On the first wall there were signs in three languages (Hebrew, Greek, and Latin) that strictly announced that no Gentile could enter beyond this point. These even said there was a death penalty for doing so. The inner courtyard was divided in a 'women's courtyard', an 'Israelite courtyard" and the Temple itself. The 'women's courtyard' was for both Jewish men and women, except those that were menstruating or just had given birth (unclean). The other part was divided in two; one for ordinary Jewish men the other for the priests with some restrictions on both. If they were suffering from certain illnesses or handicaps they had no access. Here is where you would find

2. Gerd Theissen, *Jesus. Overleveringen og dens sociale baggrund (Jesus. The Oral Tradition and The Social Context)*.

the altar of burnt offerings and the slaughter tables. The temple itself was also divided into The Holy Place and the Holy of Holies. Only the priests had access to the Temple and only the High Priest was allowed into the Holy of Holies once a year on the Day of Atonement.

We can see by the physical structure how the Temple's sanctity and holiness was safeguarded. At the same time there is an obvious sorting of people according to nationality, gender and physical status. In reality this meant that many people—most people—never had a chance to get into the temple itself. Jesus turned this upside down and said in word and deed that all people are equally near to the heart of God, of equal worth in the eyes of God. Also St. Paul captured this: God makes no distinction between people! (Romans 2)

In the early Church this was revolutionary. Notions of Jew and Gentile, pure and impure were abolished. It is hard to imagine today how revolutionary socially and religiously were both baptism and communion. Women and men were baptized at the same time and on the same conditions. Communion was open to both Jew and Gentile. Today we hardly understand how this impacted both the *image of God* and the general view of human life. Naturally this did not happen without a struggle and a bitter theological discussion. Just read Paul's Letter to the Galatians. Or you may read the pivotal story about this in Acts chapter 10: Peter had a notion of going to visit a Roman official, Cornelius, although Cornelius was a Gentile. Then Peter has a vision: Something like a large sheet with all kinds of animals is lowered before him and he is told to get up and enjoy the food. But Peter protests: 'By no means Lord, for I have never eaten anything that is profane or unclean.' Then the voice told him: 'What God has made clean, you must not call profane.' After some hesitation Peter goes to Cornelius and as they enter his house Peter said: You yourselves know that it is unlawful for a Jew to associate with or visit a Gentile; but God has shown me that I should not call anyone profane or unclean.... While Peter was still speaking the Holy Spirit fell upon all who heard the word. The circumcised believers who had come with Peter were astounded that the gift of the Holy Spirit had been poured out even on the Gentiles.' The astonishment culminates in baptism of Cornelius and everyone in his house. I find this to be a monumental story that shows the dilemmas of the early Jewish Christians as they struggled with inherited culture and tradition.

FOURTH VIGNETTE: "YOU HAVE HEARD THAT IT WAS SAID … BUT I SAY …" THE ANTI-THESIS IN THE SERMON ON THE MOUNT. (MATTHEW 5:21–48.)

- You have heard that it was said: 'You shall not murder'

  -but I say to you that if you are angry with a brother or sister, you will be liable to judgement; and if you insult a brother or sister you will be liable to the council; and if you say 'You fool' you will be liable to the hell of fire.

- You have heard that it was said: 'You shall not commit adultery'

  -but I say to you that everyone who looks at a woman with lust has already committed adultery with her in his heart.

- You have heard that it was said: 'You shall not swear falsely'

  -but I say to you, Do not swear at all, either by heaven, for it is the throne of God, or by the earth, for it is his footstool, or by Jerusalem, for it is the city of the great King.

- You have heard that it was said: 'An eye for an eye and a tooth for a tooth'

  -but I say to you, Do not resist an evildoer. But if anyone strikes you on the right cheek, turn the other also;

- You have heard that it was said: 'You shall love your neighbour and hate your enemy'

  -but I say to you, Love your enemies and pray for those who persecute you, so that you may be children of your Father in heaven;

In 'The Sermon on the Mount' not only does Jesus make it radically harder to follow the Law, he also sets the Law aside (last three anti-thesis). In other words he puts his own words above the Law. This was just abominable by any contemporary Jewish thought. It was tampering with Jewish identity and tradition.

In Jewish traditional thinking 'The Law' (The Torah) was believed to be the conclusive revelation of God's nature and will for Israel. The

"The Exact Imprint of God's Very Being"—Matthew's Jesus

Law consisted of the five books known as 'Genesis, Exodus, Leviticus, Numbers, and Deuteronomy' as well as the interpretation of these in so far as these were 'writings'. Every adult Jewish person was obliged towards 'The Law'.

In the following I will touch on a few points in order to demonstrate the extent of authority with which Jesus' contemporaries held 'The Law'.

- The Law is pre-existent. (Genesis 1:1 and Proverbs 8:22 "The Lord created me at the beginning of his work." 'Wisdom' and 'The Law' are one and the same.)
- The Law actually co-created the world (Proverbs 8:30 "I was beside him as a master worker")
- The Law is universal in principle. Given to humanity at Mount Sinai; however only the Hebrew nation adopted it as their law.
- The Law is infallible, given to Moses word by word just as it was in the beginning when it was with God. Before the fulfillment of time (eschatologically speaking) The Law will be studied and observed more intensely than ever. In the "world to come" God will be the teacher. The main idea is that The Law is to be observed increasingly as time goes by. Actually the observation of The Law is a requirement for the continuation of Creation, the nation.
- Fulfilling The Law leads to salvation: Creation of the True Israel. The Law is given in order for Israel to be 'delivered onto God' as a pure nation.
- The Law is casuistic in principle. It spells out details without an overarching idea. God's will is revealed in The Law.

In Jesus' time there were several factions of the Jewish nation who advocated the observance of The Law (Partisans, Shammaites, Essenes and Pharisees). They all stressed ritual cleanliness, the prohibition of imagery (Exodus 20:4), circumcision, Sabbath-rules, and separateness from the Gentiles. The purpose was to establish the *True Israel* and to usher in the *Reign of God*.

When Jesus intensifies the demands of the Law as he does in The Sermon on the Mount he in reality makes it impossible to keep the Law. When you compare a sexual attraction to a person of the opposite gender with an extra marital affair, who then is not guilty? And likewise by equating anger with murder. To love your enemy—who is able to do that? Everyone falls short of keeping the Law. Everyone is under God's judgement. Everyone is a sinner. Everyone stands begging for grace and mercy from God.

Jesus intensifies the Law but also sets it aside; the latter by disregarding certain ritual norms and by sidestepping certain rules concerning the Sabbath (Matth 12:1 . . . ; 15:1 . . . ; 22:15 . . . ; 23:1 . . .). He gives a higher priority to human kindness that to the observance of the Law. He puts into effect that 'God's Will' never can be captured by the written word.

> In The New Testament we see for the first time a revolutionary and liberating idea: Every ethical principle, followed in earnestness, reveals a deficiency in human capacity to do "right." Ethos without compassion becomes a perversion of ethos; no guiding principle can stand alone if it is to serve all humanity. The epiphany of this insight has illuminated the ages ever since. At the time however it was merely a factor in overcoming a deep crisis in the Jewish faith. Jewish identity and Judaism could not be secured simply by intensifying the Law as hailed by different groups, but only by realizing God's grace and mercy. The fellowship of human beings (joint destiny) cannot be achieved by a more ethical regiment—it just reveals the apparent and hidden aggressive feelings between people. The only way is through a new relationship. A renewed understanding of regiment itself; and a renewed relationship between people. In fact by elevating a guilt-free trust above any rule or norm.[3]

Jesus elevates human life to be 'God's Will' above the Law:

- "I desire mercy and not sacrifices" (Matt 12:7)
- "The Sabbath was made for humankind, and not humankind for the Sabbath." (Mark 2:27)
- "For you tithe mint, dill, and cumin, and have neglected the weightier matters of the law: justice and mercy and faith." (Matt 23:23)

There is a shift in attention away from ceremony and ritual to a genuine relationship between humans. Does this mean that all rules and regulations are irrelevant? Not in my opinion. A lot of wisdom and advice

---

3. Gerd Theissen, *Jesus. Overleveringen og dens sociale baggrund (Jesus. The Oral Tradition and The Social Context)*, 112.

"The Exact Imprint of God's Very Being"—Matthew's Jesus

for a good life are captured in the codes of good behaviour, for example the Ten Commandments; however these codes of conduct should always be tested against Jesus—his message and life. At times there may be a discrepancy between passages of the Bible and Jesus' life and teaching; for instance in the question of homosexuality—as we unfolded in chapter five. Paul the Apostle speaks out against sexual relationships between people of the same gender. Nevertheless, today as the Church ushers in a "new practice" it is solidly based on Jesus' loving relationship towards all people. It was not a surprise back in 1999 when I got a lot of questions in regards to the inclusivity issues.

Is it possible to capture an ethical principle for life; something that captures the Christian faith so to speak?

Some people try to express this through the double commandment of love: "You shall love the Lord your God with all your heart, and you shall love your neighbour as yourself," in other words make love a matter of principle. To me the essence is captured in Jesus' way of life and what he stood for; how he related to people. Now what I mean by this is difficult to express, but the German theologian Dietrich Bonhoeffer has done so by way of saying 'Jesus Christ is the only true human being who ever lived' and he supports it with 'he just lived for others'. He has shown us what it means to be a human being for others.

So, Jesus Christ as an ethical model?

Yes and no. That Jesus Christ demonstrated what it means to be a true human being is deeper than the idea of a role model, it incorporates his whole life: his way of being, his teachings, his death and resurrection.

Jesus also gave voice to many new, radical ideas, for example in the Sermon on the Mount: Love your enemies, turn the other cheek..

Yes, and not only new ideas, but also a way of living out the ideas. He lived the love he talked about. This love was what brought about his crucifixion. So if we are to find a specific Christian ethic, then we must, in my opinion, connect it to his life.

And an ethical principle like that probably cannot be put into words or a code of conduct?

The Danish theologian Knud E. Løgstrup writes precisely that in his book *The Ethical Precept*. The ethical principle is radical, and it is mute. It cannot be contained in rules or behavioural codes once and for all. Instead one must in each situation discern the nature of the claim in order to respond appropriately.

It is Jesus' love that challenges established practise to change!

FIFTH VIGNETTE: IN BAD COMPANY (MATTHEW 9:9-13)

It is interesting and choking to notice who Jesus associated with. "Tax collectors and sinners" is a phrase etched into our culture. A sort of label for the people who surrounded him. And expand the 'list' according to the gospel stories with: poor people, prostitutes, and people with disabilities and stigmas. Indeed a strange mix! Poor and disabled people certainly ought not to be regarded as bad company. However we know today that the well-to-do people discounted anyone else. They simply believed that poverty and disability were God's punishment for hidden or apparent sins. So let us look a bit closer at these labels and what they actually mean. Why were these people written off? What was the religious, moral and social reasoning behind this? We have a list of low status workers from that time: "Swineherds, fruit peddlers, small merchants, town criers, deckhands, beer mongers, ferrymen, tanners, waiters, garlic sellers ... and tax-collectors (publicans) of various sorts."

TAX COLLECTORS

This was a job of ill repute in the entire region, not only in Palestine. The bad reputation may have come from some tax collectors collecting for own gain. In the Roman Empire there were rules for how much tax was levied on various goods. However the chief tax collectors used an added levy to hire other tax-collectors. This often led to an abusive over-taxation such as we know from the story of Zacchaeus (Luke 19). The reputation may also be socially grounded. A common (honest) tax collector was poor and usually came from a poor family. This is evident from various sources of information about low income such as the list above. Tax collectors often came from serfdom or had no property or possessions at all.

Apart from this they worked for an overlord or occupational power and were shunned for that reason as well. They handled 'foreign' currency and from an orthodox point of view this made them unclean. For this reason alone it was unheard of that a good Jew would eat at the same table as a tax collector. But that was what Jesus did.

SINNERS

In the gospels tax collectors and sinners are often mentioned under one breath—and add prostitutes for good measure. This grouping has alerted scholars to the insight that 'sinners' hardly is a religious term here, and certainly not in the way Paul talks about it: "all have sinned and fall short of the glory of God" (Romans 3)—a way of describing the human condition in relationship to God's grace. The way it is used in the gospels points to a certain group of people in the Palestinian society. Two groups may come to mind: The poorest of the poor who virtually had to steal just to survive or to the people in dishonourable professions who could rig the deals in their own favour e.g. gamblers, transients, charlatans, charmers, bargain pushers. From the context it seems fair to assume that these people have no honest living but make it through shady businesses—in ways that are not quite kosher—religiously speaking.

PROSTITUTES

This was not uncommon in Israel at the time. Men did not 'commit adultery' if they had extramarital sex unless it was with a woman who was in another marriage relationship. For women however there was a death penalty for having an extramarital relationship. There was no clear distinction between prostitution and free sexual interaction in the classical world. In some cases woman were ordered into prostitution by their husbands. Most often these women were 'managed' to generate an income for the man owning the brothel, sometimes the women were foreigners and prisoners of war or poor people's daughters who had been sold or 'leased' so the family could survive. In short this was a socially vulnerable group who also were further victimized by the 'morally and religiously superior'. No wonder it created an aversion when Jesus said to the religious leaders of the time: "Truly I tell you, the tax collectors and prostitutes are going into the kingdom of God ahead of you." (Matt 21:31).

Good God?

THE POOR

The word for poor in the original language actually refers to the people who are devastated and had to beg for a living. What we call dead poor. Often it refers to people who due to sickness or a birth condition are unable to earn a living and who had no supporting relatives. The word generally refers to the unemployable, debt ridden peasants, casual labourers, freed slaves, widows with a disability etc. These people made up a quite large percentage of the population in Palestine in the first century. It was a society under economic stress; partly because of repeated crop failures and other environmental factors and partly because of the systemic structures such as wealth concentration with the few, oppressive taxation, and infighting among the rich and powerful.

What complicates the picture of the era is that the word poor also refers to the pious and humble people who lived by the Law to the best of their ability. Among the religious societies in the Dead Sea area a poor person was a member who practised voluntary poverty. All this leaves one wondering what Jesus really meant when he saluted the poor as the blessed ones. There are two versions of the Beatitudes: Luke: "Blessed are the poor". And Matthew: "Blessed are the poor in spirit."

Perhaps Jesus was mindful of his poor followers, the disciples? Or did he mean the general population of followers? Or the few in the inner circle? Still keeping in mind that the general belief at the time was that poverty and sickness were God's punishments. Regardless of all we still notice Jesus speaking with people in need and taking them into his fellowship of friends. This is evident in the gospel stories as well as in contemporary secular writings.

In conclusion: Jesus was hope for the hopeless. He demonstrated that God was a God for the suffering whatever the cause; poverty, prostitution, guilt, sin, sickness, shipwrecked on life's stormy sea. He gave esteem to the people who were useless in some peoples' eyes and by the same supposedly in God's eyes. He gave back to these people the right to trust in God, while others had taken this right away from them. He gave hope to those who had nothing to hope for either on earth nor in heaven. He lovingly embraced those who were used to rejection, condemnation and harassment. According to sociologist Gerd Theissen it was precisely this "paradigm of love and reconciliation" that made a break-through in the course of two centuries and changed what he calls the 'Jesus movement' into a world wide religion.

To me it is of great interest to understand the nature of this 'Jesus movement' both socially and historically. And, I believe, perhaps even more interesting to grasp the theological impact of this. It stirs up our awareness of what it was all about: The good news that Jesus ushered in, and what the Church is and ought to be.

SIXTH VIGNETTE: "ST PETER'S CATHEDRAL" (MATTHEW 16:13-19)

St. Peter's Cathedral in the Vatican in Rome is well known around the world. Spiritually speaking it dates back to Matthew's writings and the Jesus-tradition of this gospel. In it we read how Jesus said to Peter: You are Peter, and on this rock I will build my church, and the gates of Hades will not prevail against it."(Matthew 16:18—exclusive to Matthew).

Peter is portrayed in Matthew—and in the other gospel versions—both as the one confessing and denying, both following and letting him down, both believing and disbelieving. In general the disciples of Jesus are described as very human and very imperfect people all around. They are selected by Jesus to carry his message and love to others. On these he builds his church. This says a lot about God.

In Mark there is an even rougher tone. Here they are several times described as both disbelieving and as having 'hardened hearts' (Mark 6:52; 8:17; 16:14) and as cowards. In fact the first version of Mark ended with horror and fear (Mark 16:8). It says about the women at the grave: "they went out and fled from the tomb for terror and amazement had seized them; and they said nothing to anyone for they were afraid." It is a fair question to ask why Mark portrays the disciples in this way. Is it, perhaps as Jacob Jervell believes, to emphasize that the spread of the Easter faith and the break through of the Church is not a human endeavour but God's doing? He puts it this way:

> That the gospel has spread in spite of the human efforts is due to Jesus himself. It is he who after his resurrection has made this happen. In this way both propagation and faith are inspired and unexplainable. And we could actually put a heading over the gospel: Christ alone![4]

---

4. Jacob Jervell, *Da fremtiden begyndte (When the future started)*.

Many years before this Paul used the same kind of reasoning when he wrote to the congregation in Corinth: "Consider your own call brothers and sisters: not many of you were wise by human standards, not many were powerful, not many were of noble birth.... God chose what is low and despised in the world, things that are not, to reduce things that are ...." (1 Cor 1:26–28)

It is truly amazing according to the writings of the Bible whom God has used as spokespersons and co-workers up through the ages:

- a David who was anointed to be the king as the youngest of eight brothers while he was just a small shepherd boy (1 Sam. 16).
- an Isaiah who refused to run God's errands because he experienced himself as a man of unclean lips (Isaiah 6)
- a Jeremiah who protested against God's call to be a prophet because he was so young and shy about speaking (Jeremiah 1)
- a Saul—or Paul—who his entire lifetime struggled with what he called a "thorn in the flesh" (2 Cor. 12:7) presumably a physical ailment that no one later has identified.

God's call is not directed towards people of the perfect faith, or the perfect life or the optimal talent. Not at all. Rather it is issued to plain and ordinary people.

Back to the gospel as Matthew wrote it. Gerd Theissen speaks from a scholarly point of view about two types of disciples, adherents—those he labels "charismatic travelers" and those he calls "sedentary sympathisers." The charismatic travelers "roamed the highways of Palestine and Syria in a demonstrative poverty without shoes, staff or personal effects, only with a cape; they could authentically criticise the wealthy and powerful, particularly after having disposed of everything they owned. This all because they had embarked on a total discipleship." They were, in other words, itinerant prophets and teachers who traveled from place to place and propagated the Christian faith, and they seem to have held high authority in the earliest congregations. They followed a strict code of conduct based on the gospels: no home, no family, no possessions, no security of any kind. In secular writings these 'disciples' are mentioned also, for instance in the so called *Didache* from the second century and it contains rigid rules for the people of this group. You may read: "An apostle who stays more than two days in one house is a false prophet."

The "sedentary sympathizers" eventually became congregations. They each found their own leadership as a replacement for the authority of the charismatic travelers. At first they were the physical supporters of the travelers as well as the object of their teaching. However they had a different and not as strict code of conduct as the travelers.

Whichever way Theissen's explanation of the two kinds of followers fits historical events, what remains a fact is that God chooses plain and ordinary people with a plain and simple faith and a plain and simple life in order to build, maintain, and renew the Church of the Easter-faith. I am mindful of this on almost every congregational visit I make as a bishop, and I challenge them to think about the Church: what kind of church do they want to be? I often hear the comment: "You know this, bishop, we just can't do it! We don't have enough faith. We are not fit to do it." And I in return cannot help but wonder: What is the *image of God* we as a church have propagated to the people of the church?

SEVENTH VIGNETTE: TO BECOME LIKE CHILDREN (MATTHEW 21:12-16)

Matthew's version of the Temple Cleansing has a couple of notable additions in comparison with the other gospels' version of the story. There are 'blind and lame' in the temple and there are children who cry out: 'Hosanna to the Son of David.' According to 2. Samuel 5:8 'the blind and the lame' were not allowed in the inner courtyard of the Temple: 'the blind and the lame shall not come into the house'. How strictly this was enforced, apart from those in the priesthood, in the period around Jesus ministry is unknown, but for the priests it was invariable:

> No one of your offspring throughout their generations who have a blemish may approach to offer the food of his God. For no one who has a blemish shall draw near, one who is blind or lame, or one who has a mutilated face or a limb too long, or one who has a broken foot or a broken hand, or a hunchback, or a dwarf, or a man with a blemish in his eyes or an itching disease or scabs or crushed testicles. (Leviticus 21:17-20)

Letting anyone from this list carry out the priestly duties was to desecrate the temple. In the Qumran society at Jesus' time similar rules applied. The lame, blind, deaf, crippled, . . . could not join the society. When Matthew tells about Jesus curing the sick in the Temple and about the children shouting it is his way of highlighting for whom God's Kingdom is intended, and what God's kingdom is like. Jesus gives back to those who were sorted out the full right to be in God's presence.

Children did not fully participate in the religious life of the community until they were old enough to follow the Law. At puberty they became 'sons of the Law', Bar Mitzvah. This in particular applied to the boys. More than once does Jesus elevate the child as an example of great discipleship. He uses strong words: "Truly I tell you, unless you change and become like children, you will never enter the kingdom of heaven" (Matt 18:3). The word for child—*paidion*—in the original language used here refers to a small child between 0 and 7 years old. All the more poignant then. What is Jesus trying to say? Children in the Jewish society were counted as God's gift and blessing. They assured the succession of the family and of the nation as God's chosen people. It was through your children life could go on, and childlessness was almost a catastrophe. At the same time children's worth was not appreciated until they were adults. There was no value attached to just being a child. They were a sort of incomplete people until they were able to appreciate and live by the Law. Obedience to the parents was taken for granted and any rebellious act was punished severely. Further more the Jewish society was a patriarchal society in which the boys little by little got more rights and privileges than the girls. For example the boys were fully members of the religious society at the age of twelve. The girls never really got that status. It was the men who participated in the public worship. Provided there were ten adult men (over 12 years old) gathered then a worship gathering could take place. The women didn't count at all.

The story in Matthew 19:13 is a good illustration of the insignificance of the children at the time. The disciples tried to dismiss the women who brought their children to Jesus in order for him to bless them. Jesus, quite upset, corrected his disciples and said: Let the children come to me and do not stop them; for it is to such as these that the kingdom of heaven belongs." Jesus values the children for who they are (and not for what they may become) and he naturally admits them in the kingdom (long before they can appreciate and live by the Law). The kingdom of heaven is their birth right—right now!

"Unless you change and become like children, you will never enter the kingdom of heaven" (Matthew 18:3) says Jesus to his disciples. What is the implication of this? Several things have been suggested: children's innocence, their openness, just being small. A small child cannot claim the world's wisdom, theological reasoning, conscious belief or a life lived with awareness of God's will. When the disciples are engaged in a discussion about which one of them is the greatest Jesus breaks their train of thought by placing a little child among them and saying: "unless you change and become like children…" This means that the access to the kingdom of heaven neither is through fulfilment of the Law nor through achievements of any kind. The little ones are already in the kingdom—just by being born. Perhaps this is because of the trust; trust in God's goodness and grace. Perhaps it is because of the servility, to know in your heart that you will never be able to live up to the level of goodness and grace that you honestly desire. Perhaps it is because you surrender just the way you are, knowing that God's embrace is good enough for you.

It is a very powerful image: the child and the ideal disciple. From the context we know that a child represents all who are small, all who are worthless in other peoples' eyes. Jesus obviously hitches on to the image for himself: "Whoever welcomes one such child in my name welcomes me" (Matthew 18:5).

For Matthew the child is no longer the object of teaching and formation, but a key to self understanding for the disciples and the followers of Jesus. Jesus stresses the opposite of what other Jewish rabbis teach. When asked who has the greatest favour with God and is most precious in God's sight one of them answers: "those who have studied far into the Law and good deeds." Another rabbi says: "Those who teach the Law and the tradition, and who teach the children the truth. They shall sit at God's right hand"[5]

Jesus and the children is now as then a challenge for the church. It is about our self understanding as a church and about the *image of God* we propagate as a church; an image that either frightens 'the little ones' or places them near to the heart of God.

EIGHT VIGNETTE: THE JUDGEMENT (MATTHEW 25:31–46)

In this section we will take a closer look at the difficult phrases "eternal fire" and "eternal punishment" (verse 41 and 46) both of which are exclu-

---

5. Tormod Tobiassen, *Menneskesyn I det Nye Testamente* (*The Human Condition in the New Testament*).

sively Matthew's texts. The passage is about the final judgement, the day Jesus Christ will return in glory, be seated on his throne and separate the people into two groups. Some will "go away to eternal punishment but the righteous into eternal life."—Or "separate the sheep from the goats" as the imagery goes in this passage. Actually this is a reference to a common practise at Jesus' time. During the day sheep and goats were in the pasture together, but by evening the shepherd would separate them and they would spend the night separately.

The passage has an astounding conclusion: "Lord, when was it that we saw you hungry, thirsty, a stranger, naked, sick, in prison?" The surprise lies in the criteria used for the judgement, in Jesus' identification with the hungry, the thirsty, the strangers, those who had no clothes, the sick, those who were in prison. The judgement is made on the basis of humanitarian treatment of those in need: kindness, justice, compassion.

The verdict of the judgement leads to two different conclusions about life: eternal life—eternal damnation (*heaven—hell* to use 'popular' terminology). However the intent of the story is important for the listener's understanding. Is it about Judgement? Is it about the criteria for helping others? Is it about imitating one of the characters in the story?

Back in chapter two we were wrestling with the question of *heaven & hell*—whether it was meant as a pedagogic tool in coaching people towards morality and decency. Are these Bible passages about *heaven & hell* images and metaphors or are they descriptions of a physical reality?

The concept of a judgement with two exit possibilities is a popular thought used in several parts of Matthew's gospel and is evident in the New Testament and Jewish society in general at the time of Jesus, but is foreign to the Old Testament's world except for the latest of the writings e.g. the Book of Daniel (chapter 12). However in the New Testament there is also in Paul's writings another version of the 'Judgement' which could be termed a single exit Judgement. In 1 Corinthians 15 Paul rolls up an image of total inclusiveness in the end when "God may be all in all"—the so called *apocatastasis* concept, the thought of restoring creation to its original harmonious state. This concept implies the belief that all people ultimately will be 'saved' and with God; that humans never are excluded from fellowship with God.

"The Exact Imprint of God's Very Being"—Matthew's Jesus

One of my former students, Kjertel Grandal[6], wrote a doctoral dissertation in which he poses the big question: God's love—is that not a love for all? The God who says: love your enemies; must he not also love his enemies? Grandal researches the writings of three prominent protestant theologians of the 20 century: Karl Barth, Eberhard Jüngel, and Jürgen Moltmann in his search for an answer to the question. A brief summery follows.

Karl Barth is very clear on the point that no theological reasoning by anyone can justify any limits put on "the kindness of God towards humans" as is evident in the Jesus story. Rather it is "our theological plight to see and understand it as always expanding from what we thought it to be before," and he adds later: "How ironic is the Christian faith when its most serious problem seems to be that God's grace might be too liberally given to all, and that *Hell* instead of being heavily populated perhaps could turn out to be empty!"

"According to Jüngel's understanding love is both the beginning and the end of all. Love is a power that cannot cause harm, only change that which opposes it. God's love is totally devoted to the world—to all people. And God's love story with the world is a story in which God turns towards the dying person and ushers it into God's eternity. Love is God's self-definition in this love story. In short Jüngel clearly talks about God as unconditional and generous love."

Moltmann dispels all reservations in regards to the Christ centered *apocatastasis* idea. When he does this he credits his own understanding of God and "it ultimately comes back to a combination of his love concept and his understanding of the implications of an ultimate revelation. Moltmann does not leave any room for a discussion about God's absence or eclipse that should imply a counter indication of the revelation; that love should turn out to be the source of eternal rejection."

After this you may ask: What's the purpose of a judgement if you already know the outcome? Moltmann answers: "It is *evil* that is judged . . . Now when *evil* is condemned it does not imply that *people* are condemned. Consequently in God's judgement all sinners, those who are evil and use violence, murderers and children of the devil, even the devil and all fallen angels—in short all will be liberated and brought out of their estrangement and *transformed* back into their original being. And this will happen be-

---

6. Kjertil Grandal, *En kjærlighet med rom for alle? Apokatastasistanken I lys av gudsbildet. (A Love for All People? TheApocatastasis Concept and the Image of God)*, 7, 59, 94, 122.

cause God will remains true to God's own nature, and cannot give up or allow anything to self-destruct just as God already has affirmed its worth.

We will ponder Matthew's use of the Judgement scene a bit further. Perhaps we need a revision of our thinking? The Danish pastor/poet, Kai Munk, who was executed during the Second World War for speaking out against the German occupation, preached a sermon before Christmas in 1941 and it always gives new hope to me. I include a bit of it:

> 15–16 years ago on a pearl of a summer morning I stood in my garden totally lost in the beauty of being alive. Then all of a sudden I heard an unfamiliar sound and I thought: Well perhaps this is the moment when the Lord returns?—Later, it turned out, it was a Search and Rescue drill in which they had set off an orange flare. However I do not laugh at this nor feel embarrassed about it. I simply learned something about myself for which I am very thankful.—And I will never forget the sense of sheer joy that hit me that moment with the possibility that this might be Him. Something more beautiful could not be added to an already beautiful morning.[7]

NINTH VIGNETTE: A STOLEN BODY (MATTHEW 28:11–15)

Matthew's gospel exclusively reports there was a rumour started by the Jewish authorities saying that the disciples had stolen the body of Jesus while the guards were asleep. Rationally there is nothing exceptional about such a rumour. From an ordinary point of view a resurrection is unthinkable and irrational. Human experience tells us that death has the last word. Jesus resurrection cannot be proven scientifically, only the belief in the resurrection can. "Ohne Auferstehung keine Kirche!" (Without resurrection no church) said one of the best known theologians from my course of studies, Martin Niemöller. That something exceptional happened after Jesus' Crucifixion, something that gave the disciples new courage and confidence, something which led to the formation of congregations throughout the then known world during a very brief span of years, this is above any doubt.

How the resurrection is reported in the gospels varies greatly. Mark's version reports fear as the response to what happened; Matthew a great

---

7. Kaj Munk, Med Ordets Sværd (*Sword of the Word*), 76.

"The Exact Imprint of God's Very Being"—Matthew's Jesus

joy; Luke reports wonder and disbelief; John talks about faith. One particular thing they do have in common, though. Unanimously they report that the women were the first witnesses of the resurrection, and that Mary Magdalene (Maria from Magdalla by the west shore of the Sea of Galilee) had a special role in this. This is of a particular interest for the resurrection story because women at the time did not count as witnesses in legal matters, although this is not a legal matter. They are not listed as witnesses in Paul's account of the resurrection in 1 Corinthians 15. Some theologians see this as adding credibility to the story.

The women that are mentioned in Matthew are "Mary Magdalene and the other Mary." The same two women are mentioned in the story of the crucifixion: "Many women were also there, looking on from a distance; they had followed Jesus from Galilee and provided for him. Among them were Mary Magdalene and Mary the mother of James and Joseph, and the mother of the sons of Zebedee" (Matthew 27:55–56). This phrase shows to me that Jesus had female disciples as well. Further it speaks to the position they had in the early church, especially about Mary Magdalene's role. When we compare this to what Paul wrote in his letters we get the impression that the role of the women was quite controversial. There were disputes in the congregations about women's roles as preachers and prophets as well as their social integration. If you take a look at 1 Corinthians 11 for example you notice how Paul squirms. He acknowledges the liberating way Jesus related to the women, while at the same time he is under pressure from the contemporary (theological) view of women's traditional role in society and synagogue.

Further it is obvious the women who went out to Jesus' grave must have been very brave given the restrictions that surrounded a crucifixion at the time. There was a ban on showing grief as well as on arranging a funeral. As the women went to the grave they put their own lives in jeopardy. The Roman historian Tacitus has an account of events taking place at the time of Caesar Tiberius: "Neither relatives or friends were allowed to be near and cry over those who were crucified, not even to watch for any length of time. Guards were posted strategically to intervene should someone show signs of any pity." Actions such as those taken by the women could have been punished with crucifixion.

What is surprising in the Bible when it comes to belief in the resurrection story is that in general there is no resurrection expectation. In the Old Testament paradigm people lived firmly believing in God without any thoughts of a life after they die. Nevertheless, the God of Israel is the god of life. They lived with a rock solid trust in God's care, which surrounded them in life and in death. Getting closer to Jesus' time new thoughts appear. The Book of Daniel clearly talks about the end of the ages and of a resurrection: "Many of those who sleep in the dust of the earth shall awake, some to everlasting life, and some to shame and everlasting contempt . . . and those who led many to righteousness (shall shine) like the stars forever and ever" (Daniel 12:2–3). And then there is the poignant story from the prophet Ezekiel (chapter 37) about the dry bones that come back to life; but the most eclectic future-vision is perhaps the one from Isaiah 25:6–8:

> On this mountain the Lord of hosts will make for all peoples
> A feast of rich food, a feast of well-aged wines
> Of rich food filled with marrow, of well-aged wines strained clear.
> And he will destroy on this mountain
> The shroud that is cast over all peoples
> The sheet that is spread over all nations;
> He will swallow up death forever.
> Then the Lord God will wipe away the tears from all faces
> And the disgrace of his people he will take away from all the earth,

What does Jesus' resurrection mean to Matthew? Everything! It cannot be said any other way in my opinion. Without belief in the resurrection there would be no Gospel according to Matthew. Everything he reports about Jesus is told from the resurrection perspective. It is Matthew's goal to convey an *image of God* which inspires life for the whole human race.—In our last chapter we attempt to do the same.

R. K.

8

A Good, Life-giving *Image of God*

THE BEST ANTIDOTE FOR anyone with a case of 'god-poisoning' is a shot of good, life-giving *images of God*. In this chapter we are serving up 15 of these. We could have included more, but we want to leave it to you, the reader, to recall some of your very own for better or for worse. Perhaps some of them need revision. And if you are from a culture of oral traditions some *God images* may be of a quite different nature. Perhaps shaped by the story tellers themselves. And you may have been influenced by the world of sound, smell, taste, movement, temperature and touch in the formation of the *image of God*. It is good to remember that the *image of God* pretty much is a *vessel* with a specific content—and bringing this to the point of self-awareness is a good and life giving undertaking in itself. In the Bible there are *images of God* that are difficult and need to be studied. Sometimes different contextual layers of the Bible have obscured or damaged the *image of God*. In Norway Jonas Gardell recently published the book *About God (Om Gud)* in which he attempts to trace his *image of God*. I am sure there are books in English of the same nature.

God images do not live in isolation. They blend and merge. They are like a symphony, a colourful bouquet of images. Through the arts we get in touch with something greater than ourselves. When art does just that we may get a new insight or perhaps we experience a deeper relationship; our world expands and reveals new possibilities. A window has been opened into something bigger. The connection between an *image of God* and the arts is obvious in the following.

Good God?

(1) THE GOOD SHEPHERD

The classic image of the good shepherd is a man who caries a lamb on his shoulders or who stands with a shepherd's crook (crosier) among the sheep looking at them lovingly. The *image of God* as the Good Shepherd provides comfort; especially for people who have had a rough ride and feel excluded, abandoned, wounded, alone, abused or misunderstood. In such cases it is consoling or soulful to hear words like those of the prophet Isaiah (40:11):

> "He will feed his flock like a shepherd;
> He will gather the lambs in his arms,
> And carry them in his bosom,
> And gently lead the mother sheep"

And perhaps best known of all: The Shepherd Psalm (Ps. 23):

> The LORD is my shepherd, I shall not want.
> He makes me lie down in green pastures;
> He leads me beside still waters; he restores my soul.
> He leads me in right paths for his name's sake.
> Even though I walk through the darkest valley, I fear no evil;
> For you are with me; your rod and your staff—they comfort me.

According to the Bible and the real world a shepherd may walk either ahead of or behind the flock. When the shepherd is ahead he leads and shows the flock the best path; this way they may not get into blind alleys or encounter impassable cliffs and he takes them to a place with nourishment. Or if he is behind the flock he picks up the injured ones and frees the ones who are stuck or finds those who went astray.

The Good Shepherd guides and guards his people along the way. Without fear you are able to make your independent progress. You get there on your own two feet. Like a good shepherd God gives to our life meaning and a sense of direction, joy and fulfillment. God does not abandon us in dark and troubled times or when we have gone astray; God leads our life to a good conclusion. It is no glamorous job to be a shepherd; it is a tough and dangerous occupation. The shepherd and the flock are always on the outside in more than one way, and predators are always on the prowl. The shepherd has to step in between the wolves and the sheep, risking his own life.

A *Good, Life-giving* Image of God

The New Testament writers depict Jesus as the Good Shepherd who seeks the lost and lonely until they are found. John even quotes Jesus for saying "I am the good shepherd."

We humans are afraid of losing what is dear to us. In the same way God is afraid of losing what is dear to him—us. The Bible has several stories about loss. 'Lost & found' can even be argued to be the Bible's main theme. One of the stories goes like this:

> "Which one of you, having a hundred sheep and losing one of them, does not leave the ninety-nine in the wilderness and go after the one that is lost until he finds it? When he has found it he lays it on his shoulders and rejoices. And when he comes home, he calls together his friends and neighbours, saying to them, 'Rejoice with me, for I have found my sheep that was lost.' (Luke 15:4–6)

Author Vera Sæther[1] puts it this way:

> "Stories were told about a shepherd. He had enormous shoulders. They never asked for a purpose. They just carried. They loved to carry! Carry you out of misery and trouble."

He carries home what is lost—even people who are lost in their darkness and fear. God does not ask questions about brokenness, neglect or missed opportunities. God just carries us "out of misery and trouble" as Vera Sæther puts it. Carries us to where? Well; to safety first of all, and to the knowledge that he is with us in our darkness and fear, our brokenness, and that he will not let it overwhelm us.

John's Gospel has a unique *image of God*. God is in an intimate relationship with people as it is evident in the shepherd theme:

> "He calls his own sheep by name and leads them out. When he has brought out all his own, he goes ahead of them and the sheep follow him because they know his voice .... I know my own and my own know me just as the Father knows me and I know the Father. And I lay down my life for the sheep." (John 10:3 and 14)

God's love for humanity is the reason why God is willing to risk the ultimate sacrifice. Perhaps it is hard to believe this on a personal level—that it is for each and every person—but in John's version there is no doubt. God's care is like that!

S. S. / R. K.

---

1. Vera Sæther, *Der lidelse blir samfunn* (*Where Suffering Creates Community*).

Good God?

(2) IN THE GOOD HANDS OF GOD

European churches are traditionally filled with art. The altarpiece in Ringkøbing Church, Denmark was painted in 1995 by artist Arne Haugen Sørensen. It is a picture of two enormous open hands receiving a tiny human body—the resurrection—birth? The colours are vivid. At the bottom of the picture there is a black hole (a grave?) in a blue and green earth near a cliff. Beneath the cliff there is a sea of hot red that turns dark at the horizon and is met by a blue sky. The hands coming down from above are a sunny golden yellow and they reflect the blue green earth. The tiny stick like figure is almost extracted out of the hole/grave up into the mighty hands. Up high superimposed on the hands you see a small bird like a dove hovering.

It is hard to describe the picture without also interpreting it at the same time. Here is an excerpt from an interview with the artist[2]:

> It is not enough that you illustrate a story. As an artist you must take a risk. You enter the simple (and offensive) message of the story: Fear not! Life is eternal. To accept this in a modern world is a most difficult undertaking, for me that is; that anyone should care for little me, even be there for me at the end of life. Faith is also a conscious choice, and for that reason hope more than disappointment is the driving force and inspiration in this altarpiece. It is a vision of hope against a backdrop of betrayal and death; and it sheds light over the Easter story; it reinterprets the resurrection as a testimony to a divine reality that breaks into our human world, renewing and liberating. Or as a coincidental and unexpected intimacy that suddenly encounters you and gives hope back to you. Christian hope, understood on a personal level, with the resurrection story in the back of my mind.

The resurrection story is undoubtedly one of the most difficult themes to illustrate. It represents a core belief of Christianity. It is at the same time incomprehensible, illusive and embarrassingly tangible. The altarpiece is not so much depicting an event; rather it is invoking a spiritual experience.

Haugen Sørensen's art work fits into a long history of church art over many centuries. Work done by Piero della Francescas (1412–1492, Resurrection in Arrezzo), Matthias Grünewald (1475–1528 the Isenheim alterpiece in Colmar), Salvador Dali (1904–1989, Christ of St. John of the Cross) and many others. Many attempt to portray the divine, super-

2. Haugen Sørensen's pamphlet 2001 (in the Church).

A Good, Life-giving Image of God

earthly, victorious Christ. Haugen Sørensen wanted to crate an image that was more in line with today's world view. Something for all of us small people who one day will have a common, un-glorified death. He wanted to paint something that would help us accept our human condition, see it in a greater context and inspire faith and comfort; a picture with the message: Fear not, you are in good hands.

A meditation on the altarpiece by poet and pastor L. S. Andersen[3]:

> The body is laid in the grave. At Easter the grave is empty. Short and simple. Not until death and emptiness become real can anyone understand the miracle of the resurrection. At that point the world's darkness is overcome by divine light. How? Well, the secret remains with God. None of the evangelists write an eyewitness report. Luke almost lets it happen between two breaths. The angel said: "He is not here," (which is too obvious to the women) and the angel continues: "but has risen. Remember how he told you ..."
>
> Try read or say it with a pause. Then it inspires action. A magnificent turn around almost like Isaiah's prophecy about God's compassion for the forsaken wife (Isaiah 54:7–8)
>
> "For a brief moment I abandoned you, but with great compassion I will gather you.
>
> In overflowing wrath for a moment I hid my face from you but with everlasting love I will have compassion for you, says the LORD your Redeemer"
>
> The 'forsaken wife' is the faithless generation, a faithless humanity, who is redeemed by sheer grace. This is the event captured in Haugen Sørensen's picture of the resurrection. The stick-like figure in the enormous hands is anyone; only when we know the Easter story do we understand the resurrection message.

It takes a fine artist like Haugen Sørensen to keep the story from getting trivial. It is also an art to talk about the resurrection without being embarrassing. The picture challenges and it invites pondering. In his diary "Markings" former UN General Secretary Dag Hammerskjöld wrote: "How unbelievable—to be in God's hands. Another reminder about what is eternal—and another disappointment in how long it takes me to learn it."

S. S.

---

3. From Haugen Sørensen's pamphlet 2001 (in the Church).

(3) GOD THE LIBERATOR

An expression of a *liberating image of God* can be seen in Mortensrud Church in Oslo. Sculptor Gunnar Torvund decorated the wall behind the altar with a composition of not one single event from the life of Jesus but something that he calls the essence. Symbols, shapes, smooth and sharp make possible an array of 'interpretations'. And that is precisely Torvund's intention.

This 'wall' is found in a church that is deliberately designed as a 'nature-cathedral' which is built with natural stone, glass, slates and steel. The artist says about the wall[4]:

> Since the building on its own is all in moderate nature colours I wanted the altar-wall to sparkle with a wide spectrum of colours as if it had absorbed energy and light and now passed it on to the people of the room. Similar to how light shines through the glass cracks in the slate walls the coloured light shines through the altar wall. In the church's history there are two gardens. I have incorporated those in the altar wall—Garden of Eden and Gethsemane.

Torvund's few words about his creation leaves a lot to anyone's interpretation. What made me experience this piece as an expression of the God of liberation was when I heard and saw the three special stones from other historical walls: A piece of spray-painted concrete from the Berlin Wall, that separated and oppressed neighbours for 40 years. A stone from Robben Island, the South African prison island on which Nelson Mandela was held as a prisoner of conscience for 27 years. And a stone from Jerusalem, a city that has been the centre of controversy for many years.

These stones from different places that represent oppression and strife are here given a new context. "The stone that the builders rejected has become the chief cornerstone" (Psalm 118:22 and Matthew 21:42). What was once used in oppression now becomes a sign of hope and liberation. This is precisely the central theme in Liberation-theology, a movement among Christians that started in Latin America in the late 1960s. What happened then was a grass roots shift inside the church. Traditionally the Church in South and Central-America supported the government—any government. Now however the church was increasingly becoming critical of the government—demanding land reforms, an end to systemic pov-

---

4. Gunnar Torvund, *Mortensrud kirke—en altertavle (Art in Mortensrud Church)*.

A Good, Life-giving Image of God

erty, government policies helping the poor, freedom of expression, an end to oppression, etc. It was/is a liberation struggle of the poor.

From the social struggle arose a 'new' theological term: Liberation theology. This was founded on Biblical stories of which the most important ones were the story of the Exodus, Israel's liberation from the oppression under the Egyptian Pharaohs, and stories about the prophets demanding social justice. Jesus was portrayed as a liberator; someone who chose to side with the poor and outcast against the political and religious powers; someone who was arrested, tortured and executed. Drawing parallels between Biblical history and contemporary history liberation theologians point to *real life as the arena for God's action*. They claim that salvation and liberation are one and the same. They reject the idea that Christianity primarily is a spiritual approach to life. Liberation theology advocates contextual social action and gives preference to the struggle of the poor in achieving better living conditions and a more integral part of decision making in both society and church.

Christianity is an exodus-movement. Exodus means "going out." The Jewish Exodus is the story of Moses standing up to Pharaoh: "Let my people go!" Away from slavery, out of captivity, back to the Promised Land, home to Jerusalem. Later there was a parallel in the return from Babylon. Christianity however sees it slightly differently. The New Jerusalem is a spiritual condition in which God is all in all. Jesus—after the resurrection—tells his disciples to "go out" to the ends of the world teaching and baptizing to create a new nation of believers to whom God will be ever present. Theologian Tor Aukrust calls this 'the centrifugal force of the Christian message':

> It sends its advocates across every sacred boundary. However they are not sent into a profane and god-forsaken emptiness, like the captives by the Rivers of Babylon. After Jesus resurrection there is no longer a god-forsaken profane place on earth. The resurrected one is present in all profanity. He has gone ahead of his messengers to the ends of the world. Indeed, that is where he is waiting for them, when they finally arrive there.[5]

Liberation theology has made a point of interpreting and analyzing political events as an expression of God's action through people. They have a clear sense that God's presence can be seen in every situation. The fall

---

5. Tor Aukrust, *Tilbage til det ukjendte* (*Back to the Unknown*), 36.

of the Berlin Wall in 1989 is to liberation theology a modern day type of Exodus, liberation from 40 years of oppression. The prison on Robben Island was the site where human rights activist and freedom fighter Nelson Mandel was held captive from 1964 to 1982 (from 82–90 on the main land). Born in 1918 he is still a living symbol of courage, determination, honesty, passion for the cause, and the strength of the human spirit. He lived under sub-human conditions for 26 years—without giving up hope and still believing in the good of humanity. He is one of today's universal heroes.

The "stones of liberation" are placed in the altar wall of Mortensrud Church along with other symbols such as a chalice, a loaf of bread, a fish, a boat, alpha and omega, a serpent, an eye and an ear, with a Christ-figure in the middle on a background of golden and yellow glass.

Dorothee Sölle is a German liberation theologian. She interprets the famous words 'you must take up you cross and follow me' in this way: "Today this means: You must step out of anonymity, make the invisible visible and live with a purpose." A fine example of how a biblical text can be made contextual.

S. S.

(4) GOD IN THE IMAGE OF A WOMAN.

It is a long way to Harstad on a small island off the northern coast of Norway. 68 degrees north. Harstad is just a small town with a church on the outskirts, Trondeness Church, and it is home to no less than three art treasures, altarpieces from the early middle ages. One of them has a middle section with Anna, mother of Mary, Mary and the child Jesus who is lying on his stomach and reading in a book. Quite a sight! To the right you see the Swedish saint Birgitta of Vadstena, and to the left there is an unknown woman figure, supposedly also a saint.

But there are three of these altarpieces in Trondenes Church. Another one has a female dominance. Maria with the child and a number of relatives with their children. They are carved in wood likely by the famous Lubeck-carver Bernt Notke around 1475. The carving with the reading Jesus-boy is from the beginning of the 1500 and made by a Belgian carver Justus van Gent who was affiliated with the Lübeck-carvers. One might start speculating how these carvings found their way to Trondenes Church. And you may wonder what impact this art with mostly women

A *Good, Life-giving* Image of God

has had on men and women who year after year, generation after generation, have looked at them. Has it had any influence on their *image of God*? Given them an idea of the nature of God?

Down through the ages there have been several Marys: the virgin, the meek and lowly, the favoured one—mother of God, queen of the heavens. In Luke she is portrayed as the meek and lowly (Luke 1 and 2). In John she witnesses her son suffer and give up his spirit (John 19). Her purity and virginity grows stronger and stronger with time as does her position as 'Mother of God' and 'Mother of the Church'. As late as 1950 the pope issued a decree about her heavenly assumption. Tons of legends and stories have been told about Mary/Maria down through the ages.

Have women experienced their worth increased and supported through her? Or has the emphasis on her meek and lowly status contributed to the depression of women's self esteem?

A new and exciting addition to the story telling around Mary's persona is the 2002 play "The Star of the East. The Virgin Maja on the Taiga" by Norwegian playwright Geirr Lystrup[6]. The Taiga is a (Russian) name for the sub-artic coniferous forest that starts where the tundra ends. Anyway, the Taiga starts at a small Norwegian highway intersection as you come down from the interiour highlands. The Christmas story, Mary Joseph and the Jesus-baby have been indigenized and the story placed in the middle of a Norwegian winter forest among wolves and other animals. The wise men are in the story too. Their gifts are simple: a bowl of rice, a shotgun, a flute. A bowl of rice because everyone should have at least one meal a day. A shotgun because war is over and a hunting gun is all you need; a flute because "love will make you dance." Geirr Lystrup wrote a cute play about the 'heaven-kid', about hope and love in a cold and dark world. Translator's note: A parallel to this is found in Jean de Braebeuf's epic poem:

> "'Twas in the moon of wintertime when all the birds had fled.
> That mighty Git-Chi-Manitou sent angel choirs instead.
> Before their light the stars grew dim.
> And wond'ring hunters heard the hymn:
> Jesus your king is born.
> Jesus is born!
> In excelsis Gloria."

6. Geirr Lystrup, *Stjerna fra øst. Jomfru Maja på Taigaen* (*Star of the East. Virgin Maja of the Taiga*).

Jean de Braebeuf (1593–1649) was a French missionary to the Huron Indians in North America.

God in the image of a woman. It is not a modern invention. It has a Biblical foundation. We find it throughout the church's history. Often it has been suppressed, not appreciated, or hidden, but recently it has come to light again. I would like to conclude this part with a story from Luke 15; a cute story that has survived in the shadow of the other two Luke-15-stories in which God is in the image of a man.

> "Or what woman having ten silver coins, if she loses one of them, does not light a lamp, sweep the house, and search carefully until she finds it? When she has found it she calls together her friends and neighbours, saying, 'Rejoice with me for I have found the coin that I had lost.' Just so, I tell you, there is joy in the presence of the angels of God over one sinner who repents."(Luke 15:8–10)

R. K.

(5) GOD OF THE LOWLIEST

We are baking gingerbread cookies. This is a serious undertaking for a five year old and his aunt. "Great-grandpa's wife is an angel now," he says all of a sudden in the middle of a row of ginger men and women cut out with the cookie cutter. "What are you talking about?" I say and watch the sheet in the oven and the gingerbread men get their browning edges. "Great-grandpa's wife is an angel now," he repeats a little louder and more intense. "Aha—is she?" I say, a bit afraid of prying. From where is he getting his ideas? This type of theology is neither from his home nor from his aunt. We stick to the creed and the resurrection of the body. And by the way angels are not the everyday common topic in our circles.

In the Bible there are lots of stories about angels. Perhaps the best known is the Christmas story from Luke 2:

> In that region there were shepherds living in the fields, keeping watch over their flock by night. Then an angel of the Lord stood before them . . . . and they were terrified. "Do not be afraid; for see—I am bringing you good news of great joy for all the people: to you is born this day in the city of David a Saviour, who is the Messiah, the Lord. This will be a sign for you: you will find a child wrapped in bands of cloth and lying in a manger." And suddenly

A Good, Life-giving Image of God

> there was with the angel a multitude of the heavenly host praising God and saying …

In this familiar passage the angels deliver a divine message, and the word angel simply means messenger. The astounding part of the Christmas story is not that there were angels. People talked about angels at that time with no reservation. The shocking part is that they gave the message to the shepherds. Socially and religiously they were a group of low-esteemed people. Some scholars say they are a rejected group of people in the Palestinian society at Jesus' time, along with tax collectors. Just like the tax collectors they might be suspected of helping themselves a bit too often, which is also mentioned in sources outside the Bible. However the shepherds fit in nicely with the rest of those Jesus associated with: poor people, the sick and distraught, people of a 'small' faith, those who felt they were in sin and shame up to their neck. "Tax collectors and sinners" is a common phrase in Luke's story.

From a hymn written in the century before Jesus and worded as a prayer addressed to the 'anointed one', the Messiah:

> Behold, oh Lord, and raise up for them their king, the son of David, at the time you have chosen, God, to rule over Israel, and pour over him the power to crush the oppressors, to cleanse Jerusalem of the gentiles, to cast out wisely and justly sinners from their inheritance, to crush the pride of the proud like glazed clay pots, … to vanquish sinners by the power of the word. (Solomon 17, apocryphal writings)

Then Jesus came in God's name and gathered around himself all kinds of sinners, those who did not live up to the Law, those who didn't do very well, and who by the rest were declared 'unclean'. And he said: The kingdom of God is yours! Unto you the Saviour is born!

Jesus gave these people faith, hope, and love. Actually he gave them the right to hope in God, a right that had been taken away from them by their self-righteous neighbours. Keep in mind that sickness and poverty at the time generally was seen as God's curse, as a punishment from God for sin and wrongdoing. Jesus categorically rejected this. He gave love to those who expected doom and gloom. He included them and gave them a foretaste of God's kingdom.

Then we may hope in God too. We who do not make it in the big world, or have a problem with fitting in. We who know pain as we look back and fear as we look ahead. We who have cancer and stare death straight in the eye. His life signals that we are never excluded from God's ability to re-create.

"Great-grandpa's wife is with God," I say to the five-year-old just to bring his theology a bit more in tune with the contemporary world view; without getting engaged in a theoretical debate about grave, earth and body decay. "She IS an angel then!" yells the five-year-old and clasps his hand in the table so that the newly baked gingerbread men make a great leap. I give up. Angels are not in conflict with his cosmology. Perhaps they are his way of expressing the mysterious.

Angels, and no angels. Christmas is about God incarnate in a carpenter—not a priest or a theologian. About God's Messiah born in a stable—not in a royal palace or a religious holy place. About him in company with sinners—not the righteous and pious. This gives cause to pause and wonder. He recreates the world in his image, said someone. For the mind this is an incredible mystery. And faith joins the chorus of the angels: "Glory to God in the highest heaven!"

R. K.

(6) THE CHALLENGER GOD

I was given a soccer ball the other day; in some fashion it was made of melted plastic shopping bags by street children in Lusaka, Zambia. Most of them orphan. Children who lost their parents to AIDS. They need a help that goes beyond self-help.

And I cannot help but think of a certain Bible story that is about being rich and being poor. It bothers me almost every time I wear the golden bishop-cross. Couldn't we wear a wooden cross? Back to the story: There was once a rich young man who came to Jesus and asked him: "Master what must I do to inherit eternal life?" The answer was: "go sell what you own, and give the money to the poor."—And the story goes that the man was shocked and went away grieving (Mark 10:17–22).

This story is not outdated in respect to poverty and us. Jesus' challenge is still on, even as we know our powerlessness against the challenge. What can one person really do? "If only you do right, everything will be right" I learned in confirmation class. Now, many years later I believe this is a flawed simplification of today's complex economic systems and

A *Good, Life-giving* Image of God

structures. Or is it? Is it true that we in the post-modern industrialized part of the world are caught in a narcissistic culture, characterized by a self-centred and egocentric attitude towards life and neighbour and that each one of us need to break away from it?

Now and then I remember a meditation over this Bible story that I first read many years ago. It ends like this:

> Sell everything! Did he know what he said? How could I do that? My family would be outraged. Just imagine what my grandpa would say. And my father. And Rachel, my fiancée. Should we just sell and give away what we believed to be God's blessing? Abandon all that I loved? . . . But I did want to. Wanted to follow him. Wanted to sell everything. But I couldn't. Just couldn't.
>
> I was overcome by sadness and I cried. Picked up the cape that I had dropped. Picked up myself, woke up from a dream world and realized the harsh reality. Felt incredibly sad and crushed, almost bitter because he demanded the impossible.
>
> I left. His eyes followed me. He didn't say anything, but I could sense his disappointment. For a moment we shared the same feeling of despair. Then we each went our own way. He said something to his disciples, I heard, something about richness and God's kingdom. The word 'hard', I believe. Hard indeed! Even more than hard.
>
> At home they looked at me and asked: "Where have you been? You look brilliant!" "No, well." I said. "I just met this Jesus." "Oh that crazy guy," they said. "You have always been a little too taken by utopians." "Yea, that crazy fellow," I said . . . I still lay on my bed that night and couldn't help crying before I fell asleep. I so prayed to God that he would let Jesus come by another time another evening—just so we would meet again and share joy—instead of distress—and perhaps even share the eternal life! Let it be so, oh God! I prayed.[7]

"Be merciful just as your Father is merciful!" (Luke 6:36) is the conclusion to Luke's version of the Sermon on the Plain. *Mercy* is an interesting word. In the Old Testament (Hebrew) it may be traced back to its root meaning 'mother's life' or 'that which gives life', comfort, warmth, protection. In the New Testament (Greek) it could be a deviation of the root word meaning 'kitchen table'—the table where we share our food and fellowship. *Mercy* thus is a reference to a life giving fellowship; not to almsgiving and quick

---

7. Rosemarie Köhn, *Regnbuebroen. Prekensamling og essays av kvinnelige prester* (*Rainbow Bridge. Sermons and essays by women in clergy*).

handouts; it refers to justice and equal sharing of everything we have, the earth's resources. To show *mercy* is to cross boundaries should we believe the story of the Good Samaritan who shows *mercy* towards his enemy. Listen to Terje Torkelsen[8]:

> Worst is not an evil human inclination towards
> violence; rather it is good people's silence
> To not say what you believe
> out of fear that you mention fault
> that it is theirs or mine.
> For fear of being accused of sympathizing
> it may be dangerous to your health.
> For fear of being blamed
> one chooses to be silent.
>
> This was how the priest and Levite were thinking.
> And the merciful Samaritan where is he?

A challenging *image of God.*—Is this appropriate? Does this belong in the category of a life giving image of God? I believe so, since it prods us towards a God of justice. And what more do we deep down desire than justice for all.

R. K.

(7) GOD OF LIFE

The three women walked to the grave to face the reality of death. They wanted to anoint the deceased's body—Jesus' body—in accordance with the traditional burial customs.

> When the Sabbath was over, Mary Magdalene, and Mary the mother of James, and Salome bought spices, so that they might go and anoint him. And very early on the first day of the week, when the sun had risen, they went to the tomb. They had been saying to one another, "Who will roll away the stone for us from the entrance to the tomb?" When they looked up, they saw that the stone, which was very large, had already been rolled back. As they entered the tomb, they saw a young man, dressed in a white robe, sitting on the right side; and they were alarmed. But he said to them, "Do not be alarmed; you are looking for Jesus of Nazareth,

---

8. Terje Torkelsen, *Helsefarlige personalkonflikter I Kirken* (*Unhealthy Personality Conflicts in the church*).

A Good, *Life-giving* Image of God

who was crucified. He has been raised; he is not here. Look there is the place they laid him. But go, tell his disciples and Peter that he is going ahead of you to Galilee; there you will see him, just as he told you." (Mark 16:1–7)

The three women got a lesson instead, a lesson affirming LIFE in the encounter with death. An extraordinary lesson; firstly because it was about resurrection, life from death, and secondly because it was first discoveredby women.

It is God, life's source and sustainer, who is behind this teaching: to propagate life in a world where life and death continually are in tension with each other. The God of life, the God who gives life to us, shines through in this story from Mark. And we can rightly say it is about our *image of God*; it is about the kind of *God-image* we bring with us into the church, and about the *image of God* we bring along in daily life.

The image of the life-giving God? Or perhaps of the life-spoiling, threatening, destroying God?—the *image of God* that taunts us about not measuring up in neither faith nor life.

Not long ago a mother said to me: I feel it as a punishment for the life I have lived that my child was killed in a traffic accident. Not long ago a paraplegic man in a hospital bed said: This is probably the punishment for the life I lived.

These are just two dramatic examples of what we candidly call *god-poisoning*. It refers to having an *image of God* that denies the good life and the faith that heals instead of hurts us. We all know it on a small scale: We don't live as we ought to. We don't have enough faith; we don't have the right faith. We are not up to God's standard. In a way this may be true (subjectively). On the other hand it totally undermines life's magnificence (objectively).

I was given a cross by Iloh, a priest from Nicaragua. He called it a "resurrection cross." It is decorated with simple style paintings in bright colours: women ploughing the fields, harvesting, teaching the children, caring for the sick, and women teaching women. 'This is the work of the resurrection' said my friend in Nicaragua. The resurrection is also about the life we give away, make for each other. Exemplify.

We often make faith into something extraordinary, into something that belongs in a certain corner of our life, into a Sunday activity, into something beyond this life. We do the same with the resurrection. But it is in our daily lives we need our faith to give courage, to raise us up, inspire trust. It is in our daily life, with our daily life, we need to demonstrate the resurrection. A resurrection life will lift us across the fields of sorrow, through pain, sickness and death—in the bad days and in the good days.

I hear someone protesting: I don't believe enough to do that. I don't have a faith strong enough to proclaim the resurrection in life and death. To that I can only reply with a little maxim by Hans Børli called 'Faith": "Do I believe in God? Kind of, no, yes, maybe, don't know. Opposite the real question is: Does God believe in us?"

God does! Of that I'm sure. Jesus' life story tells us this, a story that from beginning to end is a declaration of love for humanity. A believable declaration of love because it takes in death and the forces of death in and around us. A declaration of love that concretely is given to us in baptism. God believes in us and invites us to "take our place beside her at the Jubilee Loom and weave with her the tapestry of a New Creation":

> God sits there and weeps.
> The beautiful tapestry of creation
> she wove with such joy
> is mutilated, torn to shreds
> reduced to rags
> its beauty fragmented by force.
> God sits there and weeps.
> But look!
> She is gathering up the shreds
> to weave something new.
>
> She gathers
> Our shreds of sorrow
> The pain, the tears, the frustration
> Caused by cruelty and crushing
> Ignoring violating, killing.
>
> She gathers
> the rags of hard work,
> attempts at advocacy,
> initiatives for peace,
> protests against injustice
> all the seemingly little and weak
> words and deeds offered
> sacrificially
> in hope
> in faith, in love.

A Good, Life-giving Image of God

And look!
She is weaving them all
With golden threads of Jubilation
into a rich tapestry,
a creation richer, more beautiful
than the old was!

God sits there and weaves
Patiently, persistently
With a smile that radiates like a rainbow
On her tear-streaked face
And she invites us
not only to keep offering her
the shreds and rags of our suffering
and our work,

but even more—to take our place beside her
at the Jubilee Loom and weave with her
the tapestry of a New Creation.[9]

R. K.

(8) CROSSES—DOWN AND ACROSS

We do not intend to go into the Church's art history in this book; however we do think it would be appropriate to include some information about the most common symbol for Christianity: The cross. Then as now it is an 'offensive' symbol. In its simplest form it symbolizes an execution. However, today the cross is a popular symbol of belonging. Its connection to faith and devotion is more dubious. Hardly anyone makes the connection between the cross and the theme from John's gospel "No one has greater love than this, to lay down one's life for one's friends."

But the cross has a history. It took almost 300 years before the cross and the crucifixion became a motif in church art. It didn't gain 'popularity' precisely because it was associated with a most humiliating execution. Besides, the followers of Jesus were for a long time themselves in danger of being crucified—should they be identified as followers. The first pictures and crosses in the church from around 300 portrayed Jesus with a halo around his head perhaps as a prophet although more typically as a

---

9. M. Rienstra, "To all who weave."

ruler, king, emperor, sitting on a throne. The emphasis was on his power and divinity.

In Jewish tradition no one was allowed to depict the divine. This image ban historically dated back to Moses and the Israelites after the Exodus. The Egyptian picture culture had 'infiltrated' Jewish tradition and a ban was necessary. Later when the temple was built the strict rules of 'no image' was closely observed. Jesus and the disciples did not question this practice at all. After Jesus' death things remained the same for a long time; all the followers of Jesus were loyal to the image prohibition. Besides there was no surrounding culture that urged them to do anything different. Eventually, though, the Jesus movement did brake away from Jewish tradition. The message simply spread across cultural lines. This again put Christianity in dialogue with new cultures and new forms of expressing religious devotion. It must have been hard for believers to adjust to new ways, but they did. The debate over Jesus divinity and/or humanity dragged on for many years. This put the image issue and a picturing of Jesus in conflict as well. Pictures of humans were just not acceptable at the time; Pictures of the divine were banned—never mind the obvious difficulty in capturing the numinous in any art form. It took many years before picture art became acceptable. The *incarnation*—God in human form—made every picture of every person an *image of God* theologically speaking.

Church history and art history are closely related. Over the centuries style changes with the change in popular belief. When the Christian faith became the official religion of the Roman Empire in 322 many new possibilities came along. Jesus stories were brought to far away places in a relatively short period of time, and as a result the various cultural groups began to interact with the Christian faith. When we study this development it reveals that public worship became the norm, many worship buildings were built, a public piety developed, worship buildings were decorated and much more.

At first it was the victorious Christ with open eyes; a living Christ. The body on the cross was straight; he is there of own choice and he is victorious. In many cases he is wearing the golden crown of a king. There is an eschatological aspect in this. It points to the future and Christ's return at the end of the ages. The Book of Revelation contains a multitude of eschatological images—word pictures. These have provided inspiration for many other art forms ever since. At the time it was written the Book of Revelations provided hope for the future for those who were victims of the

A Good, Life-giving Image of God

widespread persecutions. Hope was found in that Christ would return—at the end of the age—and bring an end to the suffering of his followers.

Around year 1000 Christ's suffering became more obvious in the crucifixes and in the pictures. It is not a dramatic and painful death. It still conveys peace and supremacy. Some of the majesty is still there in spite of death. Jesus is not overwhelmed or broken down by the suffering; he is in charge.

From around 1400 a total change is evident. The focal point is now the suffering, the moment before death. Crucifixes become very expressive. Jesus is 'stretched', in pain, wearing a crown of thorns, the spikes are bloodstained, blood everywhere. But it is not so much Jesus himself that is the focus—it is suffering in itself. This ties Jesus into the tradition of the suffering servant.

> He was despised and rejected by others;
> A man of suffering and acquainted with infirmity;
> And as one from whom others hide their faces
> He was despised, and we held him of no account.
> Surely he has borne our infirmities and carried our diseases;
> Yet we accounted him striken, struck down by God, and afflicted
> But he was wounded for our transgressions,
> crushed for our iniquities; upon him was the punishment that made us whole,
> And by his bruises we are healed. (Isaiah 53:3–5)

Suffering becomes a central theme in monastic life and mysticism; In time it spreads as an ideal for all to follow. The cross of the Middle Ages turns into an object for meditation useful when you want to identify with Jesus' suffering. Suffering is almost regarded as a prerequisite for salvation.

The cross has several meanings: *A charm*—in baptism and other rites a person makes the sign of the cross: "The minister marks the sign of the cross on the forehead of each of the baptized ... _name_ , Child of God, you have been sealed by the Holy Spirit and marked with the cross of Christ forever."[10] *Eschatological and apocalyptic sign*—it signifies the last days and the coming of Christ's kingdom at the end of all ages. *Sign of Conquest*—death has been conquered and life is victorious. Often used on cemeteries. A legend about Emperor Constantine (285–337) tells that in the night before an important battle he saw a sign—a cross—and a voice told him "By this you will conquer." In the Crusades (1096–1270)—the

---

10. *Lutheran Book of Worship* (LBW), Augsburg Minneapolis, 124.

sign of the cross almost became a uniform emblem of the 'Christian soldiers' as they fought against 'Moslems' for the control of Jerusalem and other holy places. *Educational Cross*—a visual aid in teaching religious history and pious practices. All of these aspects blend together in the way the church uses the cross and nurtures a Christian spirituality.

One problem about the use of art in the church—as opposed to the use of a Biblical text—is that it almost 'freezes' an event into a certain interpretation. The pain of the crucifixion becomes so prominent that it almost blows all other aspects away. In some way human pain needs to be balanced without dismissing it as irrelevant. Church music has done this for a long time. Here there is no 'freezing' of an event or sentiment; because after a sombre Good Friday follows a jubilant Easter morning. There is a grandiose quality to a great many classical and contemporary musical interpretations of the Jesus story.

In recent years church art has started to use the Jesus story in a new way. We look at it from the foot of the cross. The Easter drama is about the big eternal opposites such as light and darkness, good and evil, love and hate. However when you consider the contemporary art of for instance Arne Haugen Sørensen (God's good Hands) and how he handles the events that lead to the crucifixion, then the cosmic drama about good and evil shifts to a less 'cosmic' level—or you may say that the eternal gives way to the temporal. What was it that brought Jesus on the cross? Was it pure evil in a battle against God's pure love? Or on a different level: Was it pettiness that responded to loving kindness with suspicion, to magnanimity with meanness, and to generosity with envy? In Haugen Sørensen's paintings there is more than one theme. Besides the main 'story' (the continuing battle between good and evil) there are other smaller and very human stories about close-mindedness, bad behaviour, and fear of what you don't understand.

That same reality focus is found with the artist Henrik Sørensen.[11] He paints Jesus as an ordinary person. With a hair style, and facial expression that can be found on the street outside the church. Christ is a living human being among us.

A break with tradition in church art can be seen in the choice of motif as is the case with Gunnar Torvund (God the Liberator). He does not want to portray any single event from the Jesus story, rather some

---

11. See (15) GOD OF THE FRONTIER, 148.

kind of 'essence'. An almost composite way of integrating several motifs and their meaning is typical. Multiple interpretations, a move away from the single faceted is a hallmark of today's method of expression. For example has Torvund borrowed 'the skull' from medieval paintings and used it in a 'modern' crucifixion picture at the foot of the cross. He does this out of context. It is fascinating, although puzzling and it raises an important point about symbols: they are meaningless the moment they stand on their own. They require additional knowledge. The 'coded message' excludes rather than includes and in the context of a faith where Jesus exemplified inclusiveness and relationship the use of 'symbol' is a threat to authenticity.

S. S.

(9) JESUS SAVIOUR

In the naked windswept sandscape of northern Denmark, more precisely in Gl. Skagen you will find the home of artist Niels Helledie. His means of artistic expression is clay and he produces art that bursts with energy. He also works with religious themes. A couple of years ago when I knocked on his door he gave me a sculpture to take home: a simplified ship with a cross for a mast and a human head at the top of the mast, obviously a Jesus head. On the bow you can see the letters JS—Jesus Salvator—Jesus Saviour. The idea Helledie wanted to communicate with this sculpture is the idea that Jesus identifies with his crew—with humanity. He goes down with the ship and is raised with the ship. He is the vessel and the captain.

The cross is the main theme in Helledie's religious art. His crucifixes may be understood as interpretations of the 'mysterious cross'. In the case of 'my' ship the mast actually is carved to resemble the Tree of Life and there are hearts surrounding Jesus' head. The cross and the tree of life is a very old juxtaposition of symbols known as a motif already in the oldest churches of Rome. From the death of Jesus new life sprouts forth. After Good Friday Easter morning comes next. The hearts in the halo remind me of the words attributed to Jesus in John 15:13: "No one has greater love than this, to lay down one's life for one's friends." We understand it and yet we don't. We understand it when we think of a person who puts himself in danger in order to save another person perhaps from drowning, but it is beyond understanding, a mystery, when we think about God, the creator of heaven and earth, as the subject for such an action. But perhaps we need not understand it, just ponder it like Helledie. On the sculpture there are three teardrops on the bow of the ship, and I cannot help recall a phrase from a song by Bjørn Eidsvåg:

> A teardrop falls from the virginborn
> a skinny man with a crown of thorn.
> Touched I bow me down,
> my faith, my hope, my crown.
> A skinny man who silently suffers.
> God non-other a hand him offers
> And me? I am that 'non-other.'
> My saviour and my brother.[12]

R. K.

(10) A TOKEN OF LOVE GOD

When we care about someone, we show it in one way or another: A rose, a hug, a ring, a cup of tea or coffee at the right time.

God has given us some tokens of love. The most significant for me is the sign of the cross in baptism when the pastor says: "Receive the sign of the cross as a sign of your union with the crucified and risen Lord, Jesus Christ."

Many years ago I learned from my theology professor N.A.Dahl that this custom goes way back to the earliest church, to the time when slaves were commonplace. Slaves were branded on the forehead and on the chest with the brand of the owner—like cattle is today—so anyone could see who the owner was or is. The early Christians adopted this in a symbolic way. The sign of the cross in baptism is an expression of ownership.

So I have this invisible sign on me always. It cannot be removed. It is there to stay. What is done is done for good. I can always go back to it. It's nice to keep this in mind. It does not depend on my faith, on my way of life, my achievements. It means that in life and death I belong to the Lord. Even if I lose everything, even lose myself, my mind and reasoning skills I still belong to God. I have also experienced that it provides comfort at the last stage of life when you die. Or to put is as St. Paul does: "We do not live

---

12. Bjørn Eidsvåg, *Salmer 97 (Hymns 1997)*.

to ourselves and we do not die to ourselves…, so then whether we live or whether we die we are the Lord's." (Rom. 14:7–8)

"Do not fear! You are mine!" says Isaiah, the prophet, giving voice to God, the spirit of life and death. (Is 43:1)

R. K.

(11) THE COVENANT GOD

> Eight eyes facing each other,
> Four mouths around a table.
> Four walls circle one love:
> mom and dad, Liz and Abel.
> Eight hands hitched together
> A wave of care begun.
> What a global vision
> For the world to come.[13]

As in Einar Skjæaasen's little verse we all dream of a home where it is good to be, of a dinner fellowship round the table, filled with comfort and love.

In the Bible this dream is hitched onto God, but not just as a dream, also as a part of reality. In the world of the Old Testament the relationship to God was made very concrete, manifested through a meal. It was called a covenant meal (Exodus 24). The anticipation of God's future was likewise described as a meal. The prophet Isaiah gives voice to this expectation in these words:

> On this mountain the LORD of hosts will make for all peoples
> A feast of rich food, a feast of well-aged wines
> Of rich food filled with marrow, of well-aged wines strained clear.(Ish 25:6)

The church's communion is a similar covenant meal:

> … in the night in which he was betrayed he took bread, and gave thanks; broke it, and gave it to his disciples saying: Take and eat; this is my body given for you … Again after supper he took the cup, gave thanks, and gave it for all to drink, saying: This cup is the

---

13. Einar Skjæaasen, *Bumerke (Imprint)*.

new covenant in my blood shed for you and for all people for the forgiveness of sin[14].

God's covenant with humanity is in The New Testament linked to the crucifixion, Jesus' death, to the love that is stronger than death, to the love that arose at Easter. It is a love-covenant. It is a covenant that makes forgiveness and reconciliation possible. It is a covenant that facilitates new life, that allows us to carry on on our own two feet and live the life that is ours, whether it is this way or that.

Communion is a love-symbol, a token of God's invisible grace. I don't know anyone who has described this more eloquently than Karen Blixen in her book Babette's Feast. In the story the humble servant Babette originally from France, spends her entire lottery prize on creating an elaborate feast of especially imported delicacies and wines for the two pious sisters, for whom she has been working the last 14 years, and their friends and fellow congregants. The meal becomes an expression of undeserved grace, of (God's) extravagant goodness.

And I don't know any one who has described a covenant community in a more simple way than Wera Sæther in her book *When suffering becomes community*. It is an account of the L'Arche community for mentally handicapped and others who have joined. It is found a bit north of Paris and is a self-proclaimed 'community of hope' for those who are afraid and rootless, for people who have been hurt by and expelled from their communities:

> Thirteen small houses among other small houses in the village; work with screws, wood and clay. Industrious hands are everywhere. Meal, fellowship and mass. Ordinary in every way. And God is in the ordinary and simple person, in that which contains no pretense, but just is. In our common distress, common laughter, common prayer God is our community. He sings with our voices and hands. Every day has two lengthy meals in which everyone as well as an occasional couple of guests participate. Here everyone meets—from their work in the workshop, the garden or the kitchen. Each has something to say, or perhaps a cry or a laugh. Some are glad to have a break. Workday after workday the mealtime is when you share it.—The meal is more than just eating here. The meal is rediscovered as service, fellowship and feast. The meal is sacred like a communion at church. No one says that; but that's how it is.[15]

14. *Lutheran Book of Worship*, 70.
15. Vera Sæther, *Der lidelse blir samfunn (Where Suffering Creates Community)*.

A Good, Life-giving Image of God

In a short poem she says it like this:[16]

> Between the deepest abyss
> and highest heaven
> he pitches
> a tent—the covenant tent.
>
> R. K.

(12) GOD OF THE TRANSFORMATION

Not long ago I decorated the pulpit with a butterfly. But it was not just to make it look pretty. From way back in time a butterfly has been a resurrection-symbol, a symbol of transformation, of new life that rises from virtually nothing. We may find this symbol on the older part of a cemetery, with iron crosses dating back to around 1850. You may see a casts iron shape of a butterfly emerging from a cocoon and unfolding its brand new wings. A total transformation from an insignificant larva to an incredibly beautiful butterfly. The butterfly implies a message about the resurrection; that it may be a total transformation of death, grave, suffering, pain, unbearable grief into a life whose beauty, joy, and goodness we can only imagine and hope for. The development from childhood to adulthood, is also a transformation, physical and psychological, that equals in magic that of a butterfly. Unfortunately it may seem like it is a regression when it comes to humans; the child starts as a butterfly and ends as an adult in a cocoon. Many never get the opportunity to unfold their wings because the living conditions were inadequate and hampering development. And those of us who try to keep growing in mind and spirit sometimes encounter an invisible but powerful inner obstacle. It may feel like a heaviness that keeps us in the rut, in the humdrum of routine and in the familiar experience. What we are familiar with provides a comfort. It is threatening to tamper with or leave this behind.

There is a peculiar story about this in the Bible, in Exodus 19. I'm thinking of the story about Lot's wife who was transformed into a pillar of salt because she could not help herself looking back on the place from which she fled; from that which was. We can also become so focused on what was, on the life we are used to, that we cannot handle anything new or accept changes in our life. To take a risk and to try new things, I tell myself, is a prerequisite for transformation.

---

16. Ibid.

Change is part of life, is the nature of life, whether we like it or not. What brings about the biggest changes in our life is death and love. When we dare face death and love head on transition leads to transformation. Or is it the other way around? It may be a painful process. Change contains an opportunity for growth and a risk of decline:

> Then I saw a new heaven and a new earth; for the first heaven and the first earth had passed away, and the sea was no more. And I saw the holy city, the new Jerusalem, coming down out of heaven from God, prepared as a bride adorned for her husband. And I heard a loud voice from the throne saying, "See the home of God is among mortals. He will dwell with them as their God; they will be his peoples, and God himself will be with them; he will wipe every tear from their eyes. Death will be no more; mourning and crying and pain will be no more, for the first things have passed away." And the one who was seated on the throne said, "See, I am making all things new." (Revelation 21:1–5)

R. K.

(13) GOD OF BEAUTY

"Beauty will save the world," said the Russian author Dostojevskij. And there are many of us who experience reverence, or a sense of the holy, when we are surrounded by nature's beauty; whether it be the waves rolling onto the sand, the view from a cliff, or seeing the many shades of lush green in spring.

Celtic spirituality has through the centuries had its own particular synthesis of God as the creator and the wonder of the natural. It has been kept alive in parts of Ireland, Wales, Scotland, and Bretagne (France) and has had a renaissance lately. Nature's beauty is regarded as a sheen of the heavenly world and as an expression of the nature of God. In everything natural God is present in a very concrete and visible fashion. An ancient meditation, from "Fire from the West" edited by Harald Olsen, is a good example of this.

> I am the wind that blows on the sea
> I am the wave on the ocean
> I am the whisper of the rustling leaves
> I am the light of the sun
> I am the radiance of the moon and the stars
> I am the force that makes the tree grow

A Good, Life-giving Image of God

> I am the bud that turns into a flower
> I am the movement of the swimming salmon
> I am the determination of the wild raging boar
> I am the swiftness of the jumping deer
> I am the power of the ox drawing the plough
> I am the magnificence of the mighty oak
> And I am the thoughts of every person
> who praises my beauty and grandeur.[17]

Nature is in itself a kind of sacred book in which you can glean God's essence:

> One of the wise men of that time came to the hermit Antonius in the desert and asked: "Father, how can you stand living here, deprived as you are of every comfort from books?" Anthony answered: "You are a philosopher; my books you see are the orders of creation and I can whenever I want read God's own writings."
> (Evagrius of Pontus)

Certainly, being outside in nature is more than reading a book about God. It is meeting God in person. Many of the prayers we know from Celtic spirituality makes reference to God as the creator, and there is an endless amount of legends about animals helping humans. One of the sweetest prayers is known as "To see the Sun":

> God, you who created the sun:
> You are the sun of my soul
> And I worship your light.
> I love you
> Eternal light.
> Might I get to see you
> In the light of your eternal splendour.
> You are the king of light and sunshine,
> and you know our worth:
> Be with us today
> Be with us every night.
> Be with us every night and day.
> Be with us every day and night.

The source for this strong creationism/creation theology in Celtic spirituality is probably the pre Christian nature-religion combined with the

---

17. Harald Olsen, *Ilden fra vest. Keltisk fromhetstradisjon (Fire from the West—Celtic Spirituality)*.

Bible's emphasis on God as the creator. Two of the most beautiful creation texts are found in Psalm 104 and Job 38 other than the first two creation stories in Genesis chapter 1 and 2. We do not pay much attention to the fact that there are two creation accounts in the Bible. The starting point in the first story is that the earth has to dry up, while the second one starts with a dry earth that needs water. What they have in common in spite of the differences is the belief in God as the creator.

And perhaps I should become a bit more local and turn the attention to one of our local poets—Hans Børli. In his poetry there is likewise a close connection between nature and the experience of God. I include one of his many poems as an example; the title is "That which has no face":

> A person without a sense of God—no
> that I find unbelievable.
> Even when you just brush off
> the fresh snow from your old car one winter morning
> as the black crow shrieks from a dead branch,
> and you feel the cold of the snow scraper
> against your warm fingertips,
> even then it is a sanctuary experience, a prayer
> before the icon by the flickering light of your heart
> and that which has no face.[18]

R. K.

(14) GOD OF THE PILGRIMAGE—COMPANIONSHIP

Something extraordinary happened to all of us who participated in the 1997 walk (pilgrimage) from Oslo to Trondheim starting June 24 (St. John) and ending on July 29, The Festival of St. Olav. It has to do with human companionship. It has to do with nature's beauty and the slow changes in the landscape. It has to do with the slow pace of the walk/pilgrimage. It has to do with experiencing holiness—the holy God of companionship. First a little recall of the walk before pondering its meaning.

ON A PILGRIMAGE

"Everyone on their knees!" It was not the chaplain of the walk who told us this; it was the botanist. It was a day of rest in the highlands (Dovrefjell) during the pilgrimage Oslo—Trondheim. Many of us went on a botani-

---

18. Hans Børli, *Samlede dikt (Collected Poetry)*.

cal fieldtrip in the back country, and we had to get down on our knees to see the small mountain flowers up close. One of my fellow wanderers recorded over 70 different species on our short morning walk. Most of us were surprised to find such an abundance of life up here high above the tree line on a minimal soil base.

Many miles walked already. Outside our tents and the army-tents 'flags' of clean t-shirts, socks, and unmentionables flapping in the wind. I and another ten wanderers had spent the night on mattresses on the floor in one of the army-tents that had been made available to us. It was so crowded that we hardly could put a foot on the ground between the mattresses. But we slept like rocks. What was it that made people come out for a primitive walk like this—with so simple accommodations, poor wash(room) facilities, and at times mosquitoes in large numbers?

I was pondering this on the day we started the walk in the central part of Oslo and now stood at the first rest stop while the rain was pouring down. 632 km (393 miles) to Trondheim the sign read—and I thought: What in the world have I done—planning something like this? Then a little further down the road the sun came out. Day after day we walked in continuing sunshine and a supernatural midsummer landscape. It had been years since I had sensed the beauty of the landscape in this way, so close, so multi-faceted, so pretty. And we were cheered on through every stretch of a village and its surrounding fields, with juices and fresh baking, flags hoisted and church bells ringing. It is a vivid experience to be met with tolling bells as you arrive and to be sent off again with the church bell's blessing.

There were seventeen persons in the core group of wanderers. The youngest was 11 and the oldest was seventy-six. No one was a 'power house', but together we went steadily forward day by day. Our seventy-six year old used cabbage leaves as a remedy for an infected knee. Another wrote a postcard every day to the old folk's home where he worked, in order that they could follow his journey and mark off the daily progress on the map he had hung up for them. Our Finnish lieutenant colonel who had mountain experience from the Himalayas greeted everyone we met with the words: "May all God's angels protect and keep you!"

People joined our core group for parts of our trek—a couple of days, a week, two weeks. All together 15,000 people joined the pilgrimage that summer. And the slow journey day in and day out over five weeks left us with many a profound impression of nature, fellowship, and deep conversations; to bring body and soul together on a journey from place to place, from church to church, from site to site while we sang together:

> We are a people on a journey
> Now and then we catch a glimpse
> Of a home for the pilgrim soul.
> The land of eternal life
> The land of eternal life.[19]

In the small town of *'Ringsaker'* we were treated to street theatre and an old-fashioned market outside the old medieval church that we approached via *'Clergy Street'* on which a small museum for Alf Prøjsen is located. At the museum we listened to one of the wonderful Alf Prøjsen stories 'The Boy with Pilgrim Eyes': "The boy had dark blue eyes. Big and melancholy; it was as if he was standing outside a window on a rainy night begging to come inside and get a roof over his head before moving on through the valley on his way to the church with St. Olav's shrine."

Perhaps Prøjsen was trying to say something about the yearning for the holy which is part of every person. Anyhow we all got to get inside Ringsaker Church and we slept on the church floor. Some of the group wanted to go for a swim in Lake Mjøsa that looked like a mirror that evening. Others spent the nice evening visiting outside the church.

It is a special experience to sleep on an old church floor—in a church about which we know that it has accommodated pilgrims for many centuries, even from southern Europe on their way to The Cathedral with St. Olav's shrine. Roger, the organist, played for us at night and woke us up in the morning, lighting the Christ candle. The night had an air of solemnity about it and there was a tremendous thunderstorm. Next day in Sel the mosquitoes had a feast.

Then we went up through the Golden Valley (Guldbrandsdalen) up and down the hills. The troop was invited to spend the night in the farmstead Jørundgard which was the site for filming 'Kristin Lavransdatter' a historical novel written by Nobel laureate Sigrid Undset. Mosquitoes were in and out through the rough timber walls, so by and by most of us retreated to a tent instead, where we at least could shut them out. They were in the coffee, on the toast, in our hair. Desperation was the next stage. Why on earth had we started this walk? But the wanderers held out.

---

19. Britt C. Hallquist, *Salmer 97 (Hymns 1997)*.

A Good, Life-giving Image of God

"For a long, long time I have wanted to take a pilgrimage for the purpose of walking to the quiet place inside myself, to a room of tranquility where God speaks and I listen without questioning, commenting or personal distractions. Who am I? From where do I come? What is the meaning of my life on earth?" shared one of the wanderers reading from the entries in her journal.

The broad 'Trøndelagen' landscape came next. Again the villages received the wanderers with many heartwarming 'waterholes', county delegates welcoming us as we entered new territory, and a nicely rolling countryside with grain fields that were starting to turn golden yellow, and wooded hills. But finally we were there at the goal.

The Cathedral in Trondheim (Nidarosdomen) and its west wall niche where the Olav Shrine is found. We were several hundreds of short and long term wanderers. It was July 29th and the official opening of the pilgrim walk. Walking to Trondheim was something. Now something else was the Olav-vigil—the night-watch-n-wake in the cathedral as we moved about in the semidarkness of the cathedral and felt the beauty of the stonework and the architecture; but also the shadow images of the gargoyles and stone heads; some of them with tongues sticking out at us from way up there on the walls. The cathedral nicely accommodated many group meetings and conversations and at the same time provided many quiet corners for reflection and prayer.

The journey is complete. We were a bit unsure in respect to what was the most important aspect, the route, the lengthy walk we had together, or the destination: to actually be at St Olav's Church. Perhaps it should not be separated? The destination supplies a purpose other than the beauty we experienced in nature and in human warmth and fellowship. In an Italian research report on contemporary pilgrimages they site that people walk to 'restore a lost identity'. Lots of food for thought.

MEDITATION IN DOVRE CHURCH

> Then Jesus came from Galilee to John at the Jordan to be baptized by him. John would have prevented him, saying, "I need to be baptized by you, and do you come to me?" But Jesus answered him, "Let it be so now; for it is proper for us in this way to fulfill all righteousness." Then he consented. And when Jesus had been baptized, just as he came up from the water, suddenly the heavens were opened to him and he saw the Spirit of God descending like a dove and alightening

on him. And a voice from heaven said, "This is my Son, the Beloved, with whom I am well pleased." (Matthew 3:13–17)

Between Oslo and Nidaros we have a dedication service. We are replicating the medieval pilgrimage to Saint Olav's shrine in the high-alter in the cathedral; a trek walked by people from the Nordic countries and from countries further south on the continent. They all sought healing for body and soul, for sin and guilt.

We now walk along that trek. In one way: It is a physical exercise. In a profound way: It is a spiritual exercise—our life journey—from birth to death, from cradle to grave, from creation's mystery to God's eternity. Listen to Hans Børli's poem:

> A voice in the wind
> No, I was not on top of Mount Nebo,
> I was bathing in the evening sun on this signal hill
> and heard a voice that talked to me:
> - You, who perplexed turned around
> in dark and blind alleys; you, who covered in dust
> stood in the side wind
> under pointing road signs; you,
> who always were looking for something
> you didn't know what was;
> You must know this:
> There is One who is looking for you.
> Light a fire here on this sundown hill.
> Throw your walking stick into the flames.
> And wait.[20]

We throw the walking stick away for a moment and listen to the words: "There is One who is looking for you." We walk assured that we are being found. He looks for us, he who loves us and wants everything good for us.

We don't always recognize him. We don't always hear his voice. Grief, doubt, life's evil, our own insensitivity comes between. But he wants to walk with us on our journey. He wants us to know that we do not walk life's journey alone.

The altar piece in Seegaard new church is a strong message about this. Christ's face is hidden. It is in a blur, but we do see his arms, his hands lifted towards us as in a blessing. There was a lot of discussion at the unveiling of this altar painting: Is it acceptable to paint a faceless Christ on an altar

---

20. Hans Børli, *Samlede dikt (Collected Poetry)*.

painting? To me there was a sermon in the painting: That's life! We do not always know who it is, but we know someone is there. Walks with us.

The story of Jesus' baptism is in my opinion about the same. He was baptized like we were, although under protest. Above him the words: "This is my Son, the beloved." At our baptism the same voice echoes: You are my child, loved through and through, although in a different way. He holds on to us when our doubt tops our faith. He holds us fast when we are not able to hold on. He holds us fast when we hate our life, when we fail to accept it the way it is. He gives us back our life after we have lost it.

"Who shall ascend the hill of the LORD? And who shall stand in his holy place?" is the question in the ancient pilgrim hymn (Psalm 24:3) and the answer is: "Those who have clean hands and pure hearts." We don't have such. And still. He gave it to us in the waters of baptism. The grace of baptism lasts a whole lifetime and even into death. We may always cling to this grace.

He who walks with us, has been named: "He who always waits." He waits for us at the sunset, when we are throwing our walking stick down for the last time. It is good to know this. We will not get lost. We are not destined for destruction. We go back to Him who gave us life. "It's nice to be expected; to come home," says Gunnar Reiss-Andersen in a poem about death.

We receive signs of life along our journey. Bread and wine, what at one time was the daily menu; they are sacred. 'Food for the journey'. A sign that our journey is not in vain, that it has meaning, that our life is made sacred by the Lord; The bread of life—given for us—to strengthen, salve, comfort. And our answer in the words of poet Anbjørg Oldervik: "We live our lives—this is what we have to offer; with trepidation we lift it up—we extend our hands."

Amen!

AT THE END OF THE JOURNEY

"At the fountain I want to bend and drink from it; quench my thirst, my burning thirst for that which I do not comprehend, but that which I do know exists," wrote Pär Lagerkvist in his trilogy about the pilgrim Tobias traveling to the Holy Land.

This summer, the festival of St.Olav on July 29, and the1997 Church Festival have all been about 'The Pilgrimage'. Humans have sought after a fountain of 'life'—a *source for our life journey* from which we could 'drink' new energy, fresh courage, new faith, new passion and joy.

Did we find what we were looking for? Or perhaps we concur with Gregory of Nyssa in the 300: "My faith had not wavered before the walk, and it did not increase after the walk . . . Intimacy with God does not happen by visiting certain places. God wants to visit with you regardless of where you are."

Or did we find something else, something we did not anticipate? In my case I rediscovered something on the walk that I will always treasure in my heart: Intimacy with nature and its incredible beauty (even in plants so small that we had to get on our knees to see them), people's goodness and care for each other (even as they were total strangers at the beginning), but also people's deep loneliness. There is a journey we walk alone. It is the journey of our souls: love, God, death.

In Trondheim we walked round the cathedral and walked about in the cathedral, and we were taken by its monumental and upward leading beauty, its worshipful stone work in tune with our words and music, its accommodation of peace and prayer and its many niches and aisles that merged into a plaza for conversation and sharing of thoughts, an inner walk in more than one sense.

From pillars and ledges we were watched by gargoyles—grotesquely carved stone figures—reminding us that there are evil forces of life, that which strives to extinguish the love in us and between us and rob the human, the 'small' human, of its unique worth.—At the same time they reminded us of our daily and ongoing battle against these forces.

And we walked from the cathedral to the convention centre through the hustle and bustle of the city. So many different faces glanced at us: excited children's faces, inquisitive faces of youth, defiant faces, exhausted adult faces, aging faces full of wrinkles and good experiences, open faces, closed faces, happy faces, faces full of fear.—And in and above every one of these faces God's own face shining on us and being gracious to us.

Will we be able to keep together everything we have seen? Keep it together before God's face, now that we are returning home each to our own? The pilgrims of the Middle Ages walked back home. That gave them a chance to talk it over, reflect upon and re-live all they had seen and done together; what they had experienced on the road towards and at the destination; at the holy place.

A *Good, Life-giving* Image of God

Most of us are thrown right back to our daily life. Perhaps we each reflect on the impressions alone. But the journey is not complete until we have completed the slow journey home; at least in our inner mind.—For there are still "oceans to cross, forests to explore and a wilderness in which to get lost" to quote Alfred Hauge.[21]

Do we then put to use what we have seen and experienced along the way and at the shrine as a new truth for our daily life and our faith? Dare we bring forth the crucified love in the midst of our daily activities? Dare we live by the crucified and risen love that can liberate and lift up the human spirit?

Through our experience of a crucified and risen love the eternal God speaks to us as God did through the prophet Isaiah long before:

> Do not fear, for I have redeemed you;
> I have called you by name you are mine.
> When you pass through the waters, I will be with you;
> And through the rivers, they will not overwhelm you;
> When you walk through fire you shall not be burned
> And the flame shall not consume you.
> For I am the Lord your God the Holy One (Isaiah 43)

In medieval art Jesus is often pictured as a pilgrim with all the pilgrim characteristics: walking stick, mantel, hat, canteen, money bag. This cannot say anything other than he is our fellow traveler through life and death. He walks with us in pain and fear, in joy and happiness. He bears our loneliness.

Isn't just that the theme of the ancient pilgrim hymn, Psalm 24 in the Bible? We imagine this for our inner eye: A group of pilgrims standing outside the gate to the temple singing: "We are the company of those who seek him; who seek the face of the God of Jacob." And the response ends with: "Lift up your heads, O gates! And be lifted up, O ancient doors! That the King of glory may come in. Who is this King of glory? The Lord of hosts, he is the King of glory."

God is not only in his holy temple. He journeys with his people day and night. And he also supplies our travel food of bread and wine as a visible sign that he is present with us. No one has to walk alone. He goes with us.

---

21. Alfred Hauge, *Pilgrimshåndboka (Handbook for Pilgrims).*

So it is! Glory to the Father, and to the Son, and to the Holy Spirit, as it was in the beginning, is now, and will be forever; one God throughout eternity. Amen!

R. K.

(15) GOD OF THE FRONTIER

"Christ is risen—life is set free" said St John of Chrysostomos (347–407) in an Easter sermon.

"Christ is risen—life is set free." The same message is given in the altar painting by Henrik Sørensen in the Hamar Cathedral. The entire room is filled with this image. Your eyes are drawn to it as soon as you enter the church. This radiant energetic figure (Christ) with his hands lifted stands by the grave—or is it perhaps the globe—with a broken chain from each hand. Death's power is broken and—"life is set free."

I won't forget what one person said to me after my consecration as a bishop in the cathedral: "I managed to keep my tears back until you went up under the altar picture, but when you stood there under the risen Christ with the broken chain, then I couldn't any more." For her this event was an experience of the resurrection's frontier crossing power that a woman could become a bishop in the Church of Norway.

However there are three paintings in the altar piece. Let us look to the left side where there is a painting of a woman with a child. Henrik Sørensen has named this piece "The Predicament." The dark earth tones, the mother's worried stance holding the bleeding child, the earth stained, a pole that looks like a crooked cross—it all breathes anxiety and something awful. It expresses the mother's and all mothers' worry for their child's future.

However, a closer look at this picture reveals that the earth tones change into green —colour of growth and life—on the side up against the Christ picture—with the broken chains; and the crooked cross is almost like a road sign pointing to the centre—the resurrection.

The third painting of the three is quite mundane and trivial: a horse and a worker in a field—probably the only altar-painting in Norway with a decent workhorse. Henrik Sørensen is alluding to the well-known story about Hans Nielsen Hauge who had his spiritual awakening on a spring day, April 5, 1796 while working on his homestead farm. In the picture the light streams in from the centre piece—the resurrection—illuminating the horse and Hauge. From Hauge's own autobiography:

A Good, Life-giving Image of God

> One time I was working outside under a clear sky and singing a hymn I knew by heart: Jesus, how sweet to meet you one day ... When I came to the second verse: Give me the strength to feel it within ... —I felt my spirit so uplifted towards God, that I didn't even know what happened to me nor can I say what was going on; I was outside my body; and the first thing my mind realized was the regret that I had not served the dear and ever-generous God, and that nothing in the world could compare with this. That my soul felt something supernatural, divine and sacred; that this day showed me that which some days later happened.—No one has ever argued against this, because I know all the goodness in my soul, that followed after this moment, especially the intimate burning love for God and my neighbour, that I had an entirely changed attitude, a regret about all sins, a desire that all people should share in the same grace experience.[22]

Perhaps the horse in Henrik Sørensen's picture is a symbol of willingness and endurance? In Hans Nielsen Hauge's case this spring experience fostered a life long commitment to an extensive travel and preaching ministry. He also became an industrial pioneer setting up sawmills, spinning industries, print shops, meat processing plants, flour mills and more. In this way he helped a lot of people make a better living. He also improved status and respect for women by encouraging their travel and preaching ministries, and also supported it with scripture interpretations when his followers became doubtful of this.

His preaching activities eventually led to his imprisonment for several years, sometimes given a harsh treatment. By the established church and the government he was regarded as a trouble maker.

Through his paintings in the Hamar Cathedral Henrik Sørensen communicates the resurrection in more than one way: As victory over the power of death, and as the life-force that inspires peoples' daily lives. In the words of the Danish pioneer/poet/churchman/educator N.F.S Grundtvig:

> Easter Morning ends the sadness
> Ends the sadness for ever more;
> It gave to all the light and life
> Light and life for the daily chore.
> Easter Morning ends the sadness
> Ends the sadness for ever more.

R. K.

---

22. Hans Nielsen Hauge wrote two books: *Rules for Evangelical Living* and *Thoughts on the Evil Ways of the World.*

Bibliography

LITERATURE IN LANGUAGES OTHER than English form the majority of this list. (English *translation* of the title is in brackets). These were the sources listed by the authors. Often books written in English on the same or a similar topic are available.

All scripture quotations are from: The Holy Bible—New Revised Standard Version, 1989 by Division of Christian Education of the National Council of the Churches of Christ in the United States of America.

Exerts from Synod and Bishops' meetings in 1995 and 1997 are taken from the official minutes of meetings.

Aarflot, Andreas. *Norsk kirke i tusen år (Church of Norway for 1000 years).* Universitetsforlaget, Oslo 1978.
Aukrust, Tor. *Tilbake til det ukjente (Back to the Unknown).* Land og Kirke/Gyldendal 1982.
Austad, Arne. *Seksuell identitet (Sexual Identity).* Inter medicos, 1/2000.
Bakken, Arne. *Pilgrimsvandring—før og nå (Pilgrimage—Then and Now).* Trondheim 1994.
Bergstrand, Göran. *En illusion och dess utveckling (An Illusion and Its Development).* Verbum, Scockholm 1984.
Bergstrand, Göran. *Från naivitet till naivitet (From Naïve to Naïve).* Verbum, Stockholm 1990.
Blixen, Karen/Isak Dinesen. *Babettes Gæstebud (Babette's Feast).* Gyldendal Tranebog, Viborg 1998. *(Babette's Feast*—has been turned into a movie*).*
Bonhoeffer, Dietrich. Wiederstand und Ergebung 1959.
Borgen, Peder. *Det nye testaments omverden (The Context of the New Testament).* (Salomons salme 17) Tapir forlag 1980.
Børli, Hans. *Samlede dikt (Collected Poetry).* Aschehough, Oslo 1995.
Christoffersen, Svein Aage. *Hans Nielsen Hauge og det moderne Norge (HNH and Norway today).* Skriftserien KULT, no.48, Oslo 1996.
Dahl, N.A. *Matteusevangeliet—en kommentar (St. Matthew—Commentary).* Akademisk Forlag A/S, Haugesund 1998.
Dante, Alighieri. *The Divine Comedy (Den guddommelige komedie).* The Colonial Press, New York & London 1901.
Eggen Banschbach, Renate & Hognestad, Olav. *Kristusbilleder (Images of Christ).* Tapir forlag 1992.
Eidsvåg, Bjørn. *Salmer 97 (Hymns 1997).* Det norske bibelselskab 1997.

Bibliography

Erikson, Erik. *Childhood & Society.* 1950.

———. *Young Man Luther. A Study in Psychoanalysis and History.* 1958.

———. Erikson Joan & Kivinick, Helen. *Vital Involvement in Old Age.* Northon, N.Y. 1986.

Evagrius. in Olsen, Harald. *Ilden fra vest. Keltisk fromhetstradisjon (Fire from the West—Celtic Spirituality).* Verbum 1999.

Evenshaug, O & Hallen, D. *Børne- og ungdomspsykologi (Children and Youth Psychology)* Soc.pæd. bibl. Fabritus Forlagshus, Oslo 1996.

Felton, Jack & Arterburn, Stephen. *Toxic Faith.* Oliver Nelson, 1991.

Fossan, Gudbrand & Raaheim, Kjell. *Eldreårenes psykologi (Senior Years Psychology).* Fagbok Forlaget, Oslo 1996.

Fowler, James W. *Stages of Faith.* HarperCollins, N.Y. 1981.

———. *Becoming Adult. Becoming Christian.* HarperCollins, N.Y. 1984.

———. *Faith Development and Pastoral Care.* Fortress Press, 1987.

Frielingsdorf, Karl. *Dämonische Gottesbilder.* Grünewald, Mainz 1982.

———. *Vom Überleben zum Leben.* Grünewald, Mainz 1993.

Frostenson, Anders. *Guds Kjærleik er som Stranda og som Graset (God's Love is like a Sea Shore and the Grass).* In the Hymnbook for the Lutheran Church of Norway, Olso.

Funke, Dieter. Im Glauben Erwachsen werden. München 1986.

Førde, Randi. *En undersøkelse av feminine trek hos Jahve I Det gamle Testamente (Exploring Feminine Attributes of Jahve in the Old Testament).* Specialopgave I G. T. Uni. Oslo 1988.

Grundtvig, N. F. S. *Norsk Salmebog (Norwegian Hymnal).* Verbum 2002.

Gardell, Jonas. *Om Gud (About God).* Tiden Norsk Forlag, Oslo 2003.

Grandal, Kjetil. *En kjærlighet med rom for alle? Apokatastasistanken I lys av gudsbildet. (A Love for All People? The Apocatastasis Concept and the Image of God).* Det teologiske fakultet, Oslo 2003.

Hallquist, Britt. *Salmer 97 (Hymns 1997).* Det norske bibelselskab 1997.

Hammarskjöld, Dag. *Vejmærker (Markings).* Gyldendal, Copenhagen 1965.

Hark, Helmut. *Religiöse Neurosen. Ursachen und Heilung.* Stutgart, 1981.

Hassan, Steven. *Combating Cult Mind Control.* Park Street Press, Vermont 1988.

Hauge, Alfred. *Pilgrimshåndboka (Handbook for Pilgrims).* Verbum 1997.

Hauge, Hans Nielsen. *Rules for Evangelical Living and Thoughts on the Evil Ways of the World.* Hauge, Published in Christiania, Norway, 1756.

Haugen Sørensen, Arne. . . . *med indbygget katastrofe (. . . Catastrophe included).* Museum for religiøs kunst, Lemvig, Denmark 2001.

Hellemo, Geir. *Guds billedbog (God's Pictionary).* Pax Forlag, Oslo 1999.

Hertoft, Preben. *Klinisk sexology (Clinical Sexology).* Munksgaard, Copenhagen 1976.

Hognestad, Olav & Rian, Dagfinn. *Barnet I teologi og kirke (Children in Church and Theology).* Tapir Forlag 1985.

Holl, Adolf. *Jesus I dårligt selskab (Jesus in bad company).* Gyldendal Norsk, Oslo 1972.

Homofile i kirken. En utredning fra Bispemødets arbejdsgruppe om homofili. (Same-sex partnership & the Church. An exposition by the Bishops' task force on homosexuality). Kirkens Informationstjeneste, Oslo 1995.

Homosexuella i kyrkan. Et samtaledokument (Homosexuals in the Church. For Caring Conversations). Svenska kyrkan, Uppsala 2003.

Jacobson Hole, Magnus. *Først Kirkens lære—så mennesket? (First Church policy—next being human?).* Editorial in Kristiansand Avis (Daily), March 1999.

Bibliography

Jacobson, Rolf. *Alle mine dikt (All my poems)*. Gyldendal, Oslo 1990.
Jervell, Jacob. *Da fremtiden begyndte (When the future started)*. Land og Kirke, 1967.
Johnson, David, Van Vandern, Jeff & Enroth, Ronald. *Churches that Abuse*. Zondervan Pub. House, Michigan 1993.
Johnson, G., Norud, H., Magelsen, T., & Lappegard, S.. Hvorfor mener vi det vi mener? Analyse av argumenter i homofilidebatten (Why do we believe what we believe? An analysis of the arguments in the debate over same-sex marriages). Hamar Diocese 1997.
Julian of Norwich. *Revelations of Divine Love,* Penguin Classics 1998—also paraphrase in *The essence of Julian* by Ralph Milton, Northstone Publishing, Kelowna Canada 2002.
Jung C. G. Die Beziehungen der Psychotherapie zur Seelsorge. Zürich,1932.
Kaldestad, Eystein. *Gjennom det menneskelige til det guddommelige (Being Human Becoming Divine)*. Rel.psyk.perspektiver. Tano Aschehoug, Oslo 1997.
Karlsaune, Gustav. *Pilgrimen. Valfartsmotiv og valfartsmål (The Spirituality of Walking. Motivation and destination)*. Tapir Forlag 1996.
Kaul, Dagny (editor). *Feministteologi på norsk (Feminist theology in Norway)*. Cappelen Akademisk Forlag 1999.
Kolnes, Ralf Ditlef. *Åpenbaring og opplevelse (Revelation and Experience)*. Luther Forlag, Oslo 1978
Kvarme, Ole Chr. M.. *Gjenom det gode landet (The Land was Rich and Good)*. Verbum 1997.
Köhn, Rosemarie. *Oppfyllelse og løfte hos Matteus (Expectations and fulfillment in St. Matthew)*. Dynamis, Oslo 1980.
———. *Jesus—de fattiges eller de frommes håb? (Jesus—hope for the poor or the pious?)*. Dynamis Oslo 1984.
———. *Regnbuebroen. Prekensamling og essays av kvinnelige prester (Rainbow Bridge. Sermons and essays by women in clergy)*. Tapir Forlag 1986
———. *Egne forelesninger over Matteusevangeliet fra perioden 1985-93 (Lectures on the Gospel of St. Matthew 1985-93)*. Institutt for religionshistorie og kristendomskunnskap, Det historisk-filosofiske fakultet, UIO.
Küng, Hans. *Christ sein (On Being a Christian)*. Doubleday, 1976.
Köster, Peter. *Forelesningsnotater fra retreatutdanningen (Notes from Retreat Practicum)*. Frankfurt 1987-1989.
Lagerkvist, Pär. *Pilgrim på havet (A Pilgrim at Sea)*. Gyldendal, Oslo, 1962.
Leirvik, O & Skeie, G.. *Materialistisk tilnærming til Bibelen (A Scientific Approach to the Bible)*. Teologisk arb. Hefte 1, 1978.
Lutheran Book of Worship, Augsburg Publishing, Minneapolis, 1978.
Lystrup, Geirr. *Stjerna fra øst. Jomfru Maja på Taigaen (Star of the East. Virgin Maja of the Taiga)*. Verbum, 2002.
Løgstrup, Knud E. *Den etiske fordring (The Ethical Imperative)*. Gyldendal, Viborg 1956
Lønning, Inge. *Levende Luther (Luther Live)*. Land og Kirke Forlag, 1967
Marstrand, Marianne. Det evige livet (Eternal life). In. *Regnbuebroen. Prekensamling og essays av kvinnelige prester (Rainbow Bridge. Sermons and essays by women in clergy)*. Tapir Forlag 1986.
Molland, Einar. Norges kirkehistorie I det 19.årh. Bind 1 (Norwegian Church History in the 19th Cent.). Gyldendal Norsk, 1979.
Moser, Tilmann. *Gottesfergiftung (Godpoisoning)*. Suhrkamp, Frankfurt 1979.

Bibliography

———. *Ein Diener Gottes (A servant of God)*. Article by Hedwig Gafga. Deutsche allgemeine Sonntagsblatt. No. 22, 1998.

Moxness, Halvor. *Gud for de ugudelige (God for the Un-Godly)*. Land og Kirke/Gyldendal 1980.

Munk, Kaj. *Med ordets sverd (Sword of the Word)*. Danske prædikener 1941–42, Nyt Nordisk Forlag Arnold Busck 1942.

Nielsen, Erik A.. *Livets træ. En bog om Niels Helledie (Tree of Life. A book about NH)*. Dafolo Forlag 1994.

Nissen, Johannes. *Budskab og konsekvens (Words and Actions)*. Forlaget Anis, 1985

Nordstokke, Kjell. *De fattiges kirke (The Church of the Poor)*. Kirkelig kulturverksted, Oslo 1987.

Nouwen, Henri J. M. Return of the Prodigal Son, Doubleday, New York, 1992.

Olsen, Harald. *Ilden fra vest. Keltisk fromhetstradisjon (Fire from the West—Celtic Spirituality)*. Verbum 1999.

Otzen, Benedikt. *Den antike jødedom (Ancient Jewish Traditions)*. Gad, Copenhagen 1984.

Poort, Ruth. *Psykologien som tjener (Psychology to Serve You)*. Land og Kirke, Oslo 1965

Prøysen, Alf. Bakken, Arne. *Nidarosdomen—en pilgrimsvandring (The Cathedral of Throndheim—A Pilgrim's Progress)*. Aschehoug 1997.

Reimers, Eva & Lindström, Susanne. *Blott I det öppna (Publicly Bleeding)*. Verbum, Stockholm 2000.

Rienstra, M. *To all who weave*. Printed in 'Women in a changing World', no 23, 1987.

Rizzuto, Ane-Maria. *The Birth of the Living God*. Uni.of Chicago Press, London, 1979.

Schweizer, Eduard. *The Good News according to Matthew*. John Knox Press, 1975.

Schottroff, Luise & Stegemann, Wolfgang. *Jesus von Nazareth Hoffnung der Armen (Jesus of Nazareth Hope for the Poor)*. Urban-Taschenbücher, Stuttgart 1978.

Simonsen, Poul. *Trondenes kirke (Church of Trondenes)*. Grafisk Forum, Harstad, 1980

Skjæraasen, Einar. *Bumerke (Imprint)*. Aschehoug, Oslo 1974.

Solberg, Karen Sidsel. *Trosudvikling—en utfordring for sjelesorgen (Faith development—the challenge in councelling)*. Tidskrift for sjelesorg, Modum 1998.

Studer, Andreas. *Destructive Religion*. Werkstatt für Lebensfragen, Zürich 2000.

Stålsett, Gunnar. *Hva er da et menneske? (Who's a Human Being then?)*. Gyldendal, Oslo, 2002.

Svare, Helge. *Livet er en rejse (Life is a journey. Metaphor in Philosophy, Science and Daily Life)*. Pax Forlag, Oslo 2002.

Sønderbo, Susanne. *Studieoptegnelser om gudsbilleder og religiøs udvikling fra retræteuddannelsen (Notes from Retreat Practicum)*. Frankfurt 1987–89.

———. *Omfavn livet midt i livet (Embracing life at Mid-life)*. Unitas Forlag, Copenhagen 1993.

———. *Glæden er gul (Joy is Yellow)*. Unitas Forlag, 1995.

———. *Forvandling og forandring (Transformation and Transition)*. Unitas 2003

Sölle, Dorothee. *Choosing Life*, Fortress Press 1981.

Sæther, Vera. *Der lidelse blir samfunn (Where Suffering Creates Community)*. Gyldendal Norsk 1975.

Theissen, Gerd. *Jesus. Overleveringen og dens sociale baggrund (Jesus. The Oral Tradition and The Social Context)*. Hans Reitzel, Copenhagen 1979.

Thorsen, Kirsten. *Kjønn, livsløp og alderdom (Gender, Lifecycle and Seniority)*. Fagbokforlaget 1998.

Bibliography

Tobiassen, Tormod. *Menneskesyn i Det nye Testamente (The Human Condition in The New Testament)*. Unfinished study at University of Oslo, UIO 1989.

Torkelsen, Terje. *Helsefarlige personalkonflikter i kirken (Unhealthy Personality Conflicts in the Church)*. Genesis Forlag, Oslo 1998.

Torvund, Gunnar. *Mortensrud kirke—en altertavle (Art in Mortensrud Church)*. Article in Byggekunst No. 4, 2002.

Wikstrøm, Owe. *Stöd eller börda? (Support or Burden?)*. Verbum, Stockholm 1979.

Susanne Sønderbo and Rosemarie Köhn